Cheap Chic Weddings

Cheap Weddings that Look Like a Million Bucks

Susan Bain ❖ Laura Gawne ❖ Roxie Radford

authorHOUSE®

AuthorHouse™
1663 Liberty Drive
Bloomington, IN 47403
www.authorhouse.com
Phone: 1-800-839-8640

Graphic Design by David Mazurek

First published by AuthorHouse 05/24/2011

ISBN: 978-1-4567-5237-8 (sc)

Library of Congress Control Number: 2011903868

Printed in the United States of America

Dedications

✿ For my son Bo who inspired me to do the web site and book. Thank you for inspiring me in everything I do. To my husband Bob who is always my rock.

— Laura

✿ To my late husband Jim for his unwavering support and patience and his pride in me.

— Roxie

✿ To my sons, Glenn, Anthony and Zack, who have been my greatest inspiration. Thank you for your love, support and help! To my husband Glenn, for his generosity, support and love.

— Susan

Contents

Acknowledgments

* Many thanks to our sister/daughter Jo Ann Oliver for her support, inspiration, love and laughter.

* To our readers, fans and Ezine subscribers...thanks for your loyalty and invaluable feedback.

* For our friends who always cheer us on.

* Big thanks to Jacquie Montes de Oca for her proofreading help.

* Special thanks to David Mazurek for his incredible talent designing our book cover and web site logo.

* Thanks to our publisher, Authorhouse for everything.

Introduction

You dreamed of your big day your whole life. You've watched celebrities and Royals wed in fantastic splendor. You fantasize that your wedding will be just as magical…but reality sets in and your budget isn't quite the same as theirs.

As far as the ceremony goes…the most important thing is that it reflects who you are, your beliefs…whether that is religious or not. And that doesn't cost money. Of course you want it to look nice and you want to look nice and there are ways to do that without spending a fortune.

The reception is all about celebrating with the people who mean the most to you. It's a party. What makes a great party? The people, the food, the ambiance, the music and the reason for being there. Notice that money isn't on the list. While money is a tool to create the vision you've dreamed of…it is not the most important element.

There are so many ways to save money on your wedding without compromising your style.

We wrote this book for everyone planning a wedding. We wrote it especially for people who want to save money without giving up their dream of a magical day. That is what Cheap Chic is all about. Creating a cheap wedding that looks like a million bucks.

Getting Started...
Your Dream Wedding on a Dime

So you're engaged! Maybe you have talked about this for a while or maybe he popped the question! Whatever way your engagement came to be, the very next step is planning your wedding! Where do you start?

Start with a vision. Imagine your perfect wedding. It may be extravagant — and you may think that you'll never be able to afford that vision. But, once you know what you want your wedding to look like — you can begin the process of honing down the expenses to fit your budget. For example, you may visualize enormous flower arrangements in every nook and cranny of the church. You can easily get the same desired results by shopping for fewer flowers — but choosing those that will make an enormous visual impact.

Choosing wisely will help you get exactly what you want while staying within the budget you've got to work with. The more you plan ahead, the easier it will be to make everything culminate into the wedding you've always dreamed of. Cutting costs and doing some of the footwork yourself shouldn't be a burden. It should make you feel wise and innovative to know that you made your dream come true – by using a little ingenuity and a lot of imagination.

Making the Vision a Reality
– While Keeping a Budget

Are you truly envisioning what you want your wedding to be, or is it what you think your parents, friends and future in-laws expect? Have they voiced opinions about your wedding? Think about how you would feel if you had the type of wedding that everyone expects. Now, for a moment, put realities like a budget out of your mind as you meditate about your dream wedding. Just get a "no holds barred" attitude and let your imagination run wild.

Think about some weddings that you've attended. What did you admire most about them and which elements do you think would have been better left out? Also, think about visions of your future wedding that you had as a child. Go into detail with your memories.

Celebrity weddings or wedding scenes that you've witnessed in movies or television (especially soap operas) are a great source of ideas for fantasy weddings. They can range from wildly extravagant to intimate and romantic.

If you're still feeling a bit overwhelmed and can't come up with a clear picture of your wedding, try brainstorming some ideas – either alone or with your significant other or friend or family member that you feel comfortable with. This should help you narrow down the true picture of what you really, really want.

Brainstorming Your Wedding with Dollars on Your Mind

If you don't yet have a clear vision of every detail of your wedding, there are ways you can brainstorm to help you make some hard decisions. You've probably been visualizing your wedding gown since you were a little girl. Bridal magazines, movies and television feature every type of gown imaginable – from Vera Wang to "off the rack" specials.

What about invitations and favors? You may have attended weddings where you've come away with ideas about what you want – or don't want – for your own wedding. There are lots of other ways to narrow down a multitude of proposals to fit your wants.

Some great brainstorming ideas that can save you many dollars include:

❀ Talk to recently married friends or family members about what you visualize for your wedding. They may offer names of caterers, seamstresses and tailors who have done a great job for them or someone they know.

❀ Online bridal shopping sites are also helpful to get an idea of what's available for the price you want to pay. Look for major discounts and sales.

❀ Bridal magazines and books are abundant and contain much more useful information than just dress styles and advice on where you should spend your honeymoon. They can also point out ways to save money and time.

❀ If you live near a big city, keep an eye out for bridal show extravaganzas. Take a day to browse through the booths for ideas -- *and by all means register for great prize giveaways and discounts.*

- ❧ Visit various sites that you're considering for the ceremony and reception. Don't leave out the home and/or garden of a relative or friend for *free* venues! Talk to the owners and see if they're open to hosting your wedding.

- ❧ Craft stores sometimes offer "how to" classes on making favors, wedding decorations and even gifts for your wedding party. Take advantage of these free classes.

If you haven't yet begun a "wedding notebook," now would be the time to start one – and describe the vision for your wedding in as much detail as you can. This will be a good starting point when you begin the actual planning.

Using a Timeline is essential in getting organized for your big day...

Getting organized and starting a timeline does not mean you can't be flexible. Planning a wedding takes some patience and you have to be willing to accept change once in a while, especially if you want to save a lot of money.

First, get yourself a large binder notebook, some dividers, and some pockets for the binder. Divide the notebook however you like. The easiest way is to divide into categories like Budget, Photography, Ceremony, Attendants, etc. Use your pockets or zipper bags for swatches, business cards, and samples. Be sure to add notebook paper for notes, ideas, dreams and inspirations!

Now you're ready to make a timeline for all of your planning. Make this timeline your own as everyone has a different amount of time to plan their wedding. The following list is an example, please add or take away tasks that fit your plans.

One-Year Timeline

Nine to Twelve Months Ahead

- ❧ Announce your engagement.
- ❧ Create a budget and discuss with family members involved.
- ❧ Select a date and time.

- ❀ Choose a look and feel of the wedding (theme, tone, formality, colors).
- ❀ Have engagement photos taken if desired.
- ❀ Decide in amount of guests and make your list.
- ❀ Reserve location(s) for the ceremony and reception.
- ❀ Book the Officiant.
- ❀ Shop for your pros...Photographer, Caterer (if separate from venue), DJ, Baker, Florist.
- ❀ Choose your attendants and ask them so they can plan ahead.
- ❀ Set up a wedding website.

Six to Nine Months Ahead

- ❀ Register at favorite stores for your wedding gift registries.
- ❀ Shop for wedding gown, accessories, veil and undergarments.
- ❀ Start to think about how you will style your hair as you gown shop.
- ❀ Decide on groom's and groomsmen attire.
- ❀ Shop for bridesmaids dresses.
- ❀ Narrow down ideas for the look and feel of the wedding. Shop for decorations.
- ❀ Choose a design for your invitations and order or make early.
- ❀ Discuss attendant duties with your wedding party.
- ❀ Start your honeymoon plans.
- ❀ Discuss accommodation needs with out of town guests. Reserve rooms if needed.
- ❀ Inquire about marriage license and apply for one.
- ❀ Make your reception food plans.

Four to Six Months Ahead

❧ Choose your wedding rings.

❧ Order the men's attire.

❧ Have mothers choose their attire.

❧ Make transportation plans. Reserve as needed.

❧ Decide whether or not you will have favors. Start making or order.

❧ Finalize honeymoon plans.

❧ Finalize any contracts with your team/vendors.

❧ Make plans/reserve for rehearsal night and dinner.

❧ Address Invitations, create any maps or inserts and include in envelopes.

❧ Reserve any rentals needed including tables, chairs, tents, dishes, etc.

❧ Plan any showers or parties that are close to the wedding date.

❧ Shop for wedding props like the cake knife, garter, ring pillow and toasting glasses.

❧ Reserve wedding night room for yourself (if you are staying local on the wedding night).

One to Three Months Ahead

❧ Finalize attendant's attire.

❧ Confirm all of your vendors (Baker, Photographer, DJ, Officiant, et al.).

❧ Finalize transportation needs.

❧ Make or buy a guest book.

❧ Shop for gifts for attendants or make your own.

❧ Attend dress fittings according to your store's schedule. Have lingerie with you.

❧ Book your hairstylists and makeup person if using one.

❧ Create and print your programs.

- ✿ Mail invitations 6 weeks ahead and keep track of responses.
- ✿ Let Officiant know about rehearsal time and place.
- ✿ Pick up marriage license if ready.
- ✿ Write any thank you notes for gifts received so far.
- ✿ Plan reception seating.
- ✿ Prepare or purchase gifts for each other.
- ✿ Look into changing official documents like driver's license, bank accounts, insurance, etc.
- ✿ Schedule final fittings for the bride and bridesmaids.

Two to Three Weeks Ahead

- ✿ Reconfirm all hotel rooms for guests and your wedding night room.
- ✿ Discuss music list with DJ/Band and Ceremony musicians/ singers.
- ✿ Check in with Officiant with any last minute questions or plans.
- ✿ Check that all attire is in place and ready to go.
- ✿ Contact any guests who have not responded so you can begin final count.
- ✿ Touch base with any vendors as needed.
- ✿ Discuss shot list with your photographer.
- ✿ Give out any maps or directions as needed.
- ✿ Finalize rehearsal and dinner plans.

One Week Ahead

- ✿ Turn in final guest count to Caterer/Hotel/Restaurant/Hall.
- ✿ Finalize any and all seating arrangements.
- ✿ Arrange for someone (i.e. Best Man) to bring wedding gifts to your home.
- ✿ Pre arrange for groom or parents to have final checks and tips ready on the wedding day.

- ❀ Begin packing for your wedding night and honeymoon.
- ❀ Finish place cards if using.
- ❀ Gather together all wedding attire and be sure everyone fits in his or her attire.
- ❀ Have rehearsal and dinner.
- ❀ Distribute gifts to attendants, parents, each other.
- ❀ Organize details for getting all rentals returned.

The Day Before

- ❀ Have your manicure, pedicure, massage.
- ❀ Pull together any last minute details and don't be afraid to ask for help!
- ❀ Relax and Get a good night's sleep!

Wedding Day

- ❀ Have a good breakfast.
- ❀ Have your hair and makeup done.
- ❀ Allow a lot of time to get dressed (2 Hours if you can).
- ❀ Bring your Wedding Back Up Bag everywhere you go.
- ❀ Be sure groom has rings and marriage license.

Right After the Wedding

- ❀ Donate any leftover flowers/plants or give away to family and friends.
- ❀ Write thank you notes to all of your wedding helpers.
- ❀ Clean and store your bridal apparel.
- ❀ Return tuxedos.

Don't get overwhelmed by this list! Remember to ask for help from your groom, family and friends. They will definitely want to help! You don't have to do it all!

Creating a Budget

Now is the time to talk to your fiancé about the expectations that you both envision for your wedding. While you're talking about expectations, it's a good idea to write down some of the elements that you both feel are *most* important to the success of your wedding -- as you both see it.

You want to consider what you can really afford to spend on your wedding! You don't want to start your married life in debt and you don't want to put parents or anyone else in debt by helping you.

You may waffle back and forth between putting more emphasis (and money) on one component of your wedding than another – and you may change your mind several times as you go along.

Divide your expenses up by percentages. Most couples spend 40 to 48% of their budget on the reception with everything else being much smaller percentages.

The exercise of dividing each aspect of your wedding and assigning a percentage of your budget to it will give you a good idea of which areas are most important to you. Your priorities are most important here. You may find that music or food or the dress is your top priority, that's how you determine where the money goes.

You and your fiancé should meet with both sets of parents. Speak directly of your expectations and responsibilities for the wedding you envision and speak frankly about the budget you have to work with. Ask them if they can contribute to the wedding expenses and be open to what the answers may be. Be sensitive to each family's privacy and financial situation.

Revamp your original budget periodically. You may decide on a wedding item that will be less (or more) money than you budgeted for, thus requiring you to put excess dollars in another area or save more in another. Keep close tabs on what you are spending and how much is left in the budget as you go through planning.

There has been a lot written about who pays for what in traditional weddings. Times have changed and there is less and less burden on only one family to pay for the bulk of the wedding. Financial help is usually dictated by who is able to help at the time. Often, Brides and Grooms contribute the most. Everyone's situation is different.

The only rule that has stuck around as far as who pays for what is that attendants generally pay for their own wedding attire, i.e. bridesmaids dresses, groomsmen tuxedos, and child attendants dresses and tuxes, including all accessories.

If you have a lot of time before the wedding date, start saving now to put any extra money towards the wedding. Pick up an extra job, extra hours, have a garage sale, cut out some of that expensive coffee…do whatever it takes to start your lives together without big debt!

Here are some things you may want to include in your budget:

- ❀ Ceremony expenses (Officiant, Venue Donation, License)
- ❀ Attire (Bridal Gown, Groom Tux, Accessories)
- ❀ Transportation
- ❀ Rings
- ❀ Stationery (Invites, Programs, Inserts, Place Cards, Stamps)
- ❀ Reception (Venue, Decorations, Food, Beverages, Cake)
- ❀ Music/Entertainment (for Ceremony and Reception)
- ❀ Flowers
- ❀ Favors
- ❀ Photography and Videography
- ❀ Gifts (for Wedding Party, Parents, Each Other)
- ❀ Wedding Day Props (Ring Pillow, Guest Book, Flower Girl Basket, Cake Knife, Candles)
- ❀ Hairstyling and Makeup
- ❀ Tips
- ❀ Wedding Night Room

Be sure to keep your Budget and Timeline in your Wedding Notebook and Take it everywhere you go!

Choosing a Date and Time

Choosing your wedding date and time is a big decision that should be made as early as possible. It is crucial for planning pretty much everything! The date you choose will be your anniversary forever. It should be special to you both.

When you sit down to discuss a date and time you may want to grab a couple of helpful tools like a calendar with all holidays on it and a Farmer's Almanac. The calendar will help you determine whether or not you wish to plan your big day near a holiday or not. The Farmer's Almanac will help you consider weather conditions for the time you are planning.

The most popular month to marry is June and second place goes to August. Other popular months are September, October and May. Months and/or seasons can play an important role in your decision-making as a season can dictate the flowers used, the tone of the wedding and the weather depending on where you live.

Choosing the month also includes how much time you are allowing for planning your wedding. Of course, the more time you have, the easier it is to save money in many instances. Finding the right bargain can take time and patience, so keep this in mind. You may not need the average 12 months to plan a small wedding with simple details.

Choosing a date near or on a holiday has its pros and cons. Holidays can be a burden to some family members and friends or it can be easier on them. Take that into consideration when planning. Religious holidays can actually hold people back from traveling to your wedding. One of the upsides to planning a seasonal or holiday wedding is that it can help you with choosing a color scheme or theme. Some people have a tough time coming up with these ideas and it really helps to use a classic theme like fall colors, Christmas décor, Halloween costumes, or spring flowers. Remember that some holidays automatically come with higher prices, like flowers on Valentine's or Mother's Day.

What day of the week is best? Saturday is the most popular day of the week to get married. While it is usually the most convenient for everyone involved, it remains the most expensive day of any given week. Reception sites, Caterers, Photographers and other vendors charge more on Saturdays and it is often difficult to book a desired weekend. If you are looking to save a big chunk of money, this is one place to do it. Booking your wedding on a Friday or Sunday or even a weekday can save hundreds or even thousands of dollars. Vendors are more likely to negotiate off days.

Saturday may be your only choice if it works best for family and guests. There are lots of other ways to save on your big day.

It is also important to choose the time of day you would like to get married. If you plan on marrying in a house of worship or restaurant or anywhere that has specific rules, you may not have a choice, as they will dictate the time. Afternoon weddings are the most popular, but that does not stop you from planning a breakfast wedding, or late night wedding. You can do whatever suits you. If you want to save big on food, you might think about having a reception that does not include dinner. If you are planning on your wedding being held at someone's home or a place like a park or museum, you will find the time is more flexible.

One last tip to help decide on a date… you may want to stay away from Daylight Savings Time days, big sports events like Super Bowl Weekend, World Series Week and the Final Four. Remember that Holidays can go either way, so give it some thought.

Wedding Attendants

Choosing people to stand up at your wedding requires careful consideration. Of course you want everyone in your wedding party to be your nearest and dearest friends and family members. These people should be your best supporters and be willing to stick with you through the process.

A good way to start thinking of who will be in the wedding is to consider your budget. While the attendants traditionally pay for their own attire and travel expenses, the larger this group is, the more it can cost you. Cutting this group down to a minimum could save you hundreds of dollars because you will need less flowers, less transportation, less rehearsal dinners, you get the idea. From the attendants' point of view, it's a good idea to talk openly with your attendants when you ask them to be in the wedding about whether or not they can afford to spend the money it takes to participate.

Attendants should be folks you can rely on, trust and those who are willing to help all the way until the big day. The number of people you decide to use in the wedding is totally up to you. Many couples are choosing to have no attendants at all, and that's perfectly fine too!

Traditional Roles of the Wedding Party

Maid/Matron of Honor - Puts together Bridal Shower, Bachelorette Party. Aides in Bride's attire shopping. Helps with Invitations. Helps Bride get dressed on wedding day. Hold's the groom's ring, if necessary. Signs the Marriage License. Helps throughout ceremony holding bouquet and assisting bride as needed

Best Man - Plans bachelor party. Responsible for the bride's ring(s) if necessary. In charge of bringing the marriage license. Assists groom in getting ready for wedding. Signs the marriage license. Oversees ushers Pays Officiant and vendors as needed Makes a toast at the reception. Ensures gifts are gathered and taken home. Transports groom/couple as needed.

Bridesmaids - Help with pre-wedding parties like the shower and bachelorette party. Assist bride with planning as needed. Aides Bride and Maid of Honor during dressing time.

Groomsmen/Ushers - Sometimes there are Groomsmen and additional Ushers. Sometimes the Groomsmen are the Ushers. They help with the bachelor party. Distribute programs. Help guests to their seats. Help guests to cocktail/reception area or to photograph area. Decorate getaway car.

Flower Girl - Is usually around 3 to 8 years old. Attends rehearsal. Comes dressed in advance of the ceremony, then walks down the aisle carrying flower petals in a basket then throws them as she walks the aisle during the ceremony. Some couples use more than one.

Ring Bearer - Is usually about 3 to 8 years old. Attends rehearsal. Comes dressed in advance of the ceremony. He carries the rings (real or fake) on a pillow down the aisle during the ceremony. Some couples use more than one.

Parents - They support their daughter and son throughout the process. Help prepare guest list. Help in shopping for attire. Make accommodations for guests. Plan pre-wedding parties. Wear attire that complements the bride/groom/theme.

Special Attendants - Don't forget that some of your family members and friends can participate by doing a single job. Have someone sing, recite a poem, do a reading, play a song, or make a toast. Some couples wouldn't think of excluding their beloved pet(s). They can walk down the aisle like everyone else, of course with a little help!

The Guest List

Creating your wedding guest list, and keeping the list down can be your biggest cost cutting exercise in the wedding planning process. It can also make for power struggles and hurt feelings. When you and your fiancé sit down to make your guest list you must keep your budget in mind and remember that just because someone is paying a big portion of the bill, it doesn't mean they can dictate the guest list. Set your goals and be strong!

Here are some tips to think about while creating your guest list:

- ❀ Start by creating a master list of everyone you would like to invite, if you could invite anyone at all.

- ❀ Divide up the head count. For instance, 50% of the list could be for the Bride and Groom and 25% to each side of the family. Or you can divide in thirds. Choose what's right for you.

- ❀ You can also prioritize your list by putting family and closest friends on the must have list and distant relatives and acquaintances on the next tier and perhaps co-workers and book club friends on the bottom of the list. This makes it easier to cut from the bottom.

- ❀ Are you going to include children? Whole families?

- ❀ One way to cut costs is to not allow single folks to bring a date or a "+1"

- When you look at the guest list, are there people on there that you have had no contact with for one, two years? You may want to cut them.
- Be sure to invite the Officiant and a guest.
- You can count on about 10% to 20% of your invited guests to send regrets.

This is probably going to be rough for the two of you, so expect that and try to be patient and understanding. Some people opt to have a very small wedding to avoid these issues. Some have a small wedding and then a big party for all friends. This your day and you want all of those in attendance to be those who mean the most to you.

The bottom line where budget is concerned is that the more people you invite, the more your wedding will cost! It's all about head count...price per person includes food, beverages, an invitation, and decorations.

Location, Location, Location

You'll be Pleasantly Surprised to know that some venues are FREE for the asking!

Where, oh where -- should your wedding be held? The answer to this question will determine where a major portion of your budget will be spent - or saved. Thinking outside the norm about the location for your wedding ceremony can save you lots of money and perhaps provide you with a stunning venue that may even surpass your vision.

Before you consider possible ceremony locations you need to think about the size of your wedding, your own site preferences and, of course, your budget. Timing the ceremony is also important. Will it be held during the day or evening? Also, will the season have an impact on the availability of the site? (Spring and summer weddings are very popular.)

If you're choosing a destination wedding, find out from the hotel or resort where the ceremony will be held. Many places have gazebos and seating in incredibly scenic settings. Booking your ceremony in a house of worship will also involve scheduling an Officiant and possibly others to assist in the preparations. Also ask about fees that you may need to include in the overall cost of the site.

When choosing a location for the ceremony, you'll also need to determine where the reception will be held. It shouldn't be so far from the ceremony that it becomes difficult or time-consuming for your guests.

If you really want to save money on the venue of your wedding ceremony and put your dollars into another portion of your wedding, think outside the box. Don't limit yourself to traditional locations simply because that's all you've ever experienced. *Be adventurous!*

Don't Overlook Extremely Affordable Wedding Venues

Affordable options that are available for your wedding ceremony are numerous and varying. If you gather all the information that you can - from the sublime to the ridiculous, it shouldn't be difficult to sit down with your fiancé and make a decision that will make you both happy.

After you've decided on the country, state and city, town or village where you want your ceremony to take place, you can begin to search for the actual location.

Some sources to consider when you begin your search (especially if you're unfamiliar with the area) include the Chamber of Commerce, Historical Societies, Local Parks and Recreation Departments and the Internet.

In all cases, be sure to ask about rules, fees and available dates. Some venues (such as a park) may have a contact person who can provide you with other information that will be pertinent to your wedding ceremony (for example, set up and clean up requirements).

Thinking out of the box means you must broaden your horizons and brainstorm alternative answers for your wedding ceremony's site. What do you and your fiancé enjoy - hiking, meeting friends at a favorite watering hole, museums and art galleries?

Here are some examples of not so expensive - and even *free* places you may want to consider:

- ❧ An art gallery or museum.
- ❧ A local college or university campus.
- ❧ Botanical garden or exotic greenhouse or rooftop garden.
- ❧ A zoo or park.
- ❧ Historical building or house.
- ❧ Building with an interesting lobby or architectural design.
- ❧ Favorite restaurant or bar.
- ❧ A scenic spot in your city or town (consider a field of flowers, mountaintop location or beach).
- ❧ Local winery.

If you're considering one of the above venues, be sure and get all the details you can from whoever is in charge of coordinating events. You may find that the rules are too stringent or that the available time frame just won't fit your schedule.

Some of these venues are absolutely **FREE** and can provide the exact backdrop you envision for your ceremony.

Inside or Outside?

The weather is the most important consideration if you're dreaming of an outdoor wedding. There's no way to predict it, but if you're planning your ceremony in an area where the weather is volatile during the season of your wedding, think twice about having it outside – or have an alternate plan. Many venues have indoor areas to use for backup.

If your heart is set on having an outside ceremony, consider changing the date of your wedding if it's set for the middle of a sun-baking summer or a typical rainy season.

Ceremonies held inside could be romantic if planned correctly. You can use inexpensive candles and romantic decorations to set an intimate mood and it won't matter what the weather is up to.

Indoor ceremonies are usually perfect for traditional weddings and these settings will probably be equipped with chairs, air conditioning, heating, lighting choices and other items you might need or want.

Think "Resources" to Trim Your Wedding Budget

Who, in your address book or business connections, might have access to the perfect venue for your wedding ceremony? Does someone you know have a membership in a private club or organization that might provide the setting you've dreamed about?

Consider the following resources when choosing a venue for your wedding:

- ❀ Your alma mater – there may be a building or place on campus that would be a perfect wedding site.
- ❀ Professional organizations – pull in favors and ask for what you want.
- ❀ Friends and family – someone you know may have a home or garden – or boat -- that they would be honored to provide for your wedding ceremony.

- Clubhouse in your apartment or condominium complex – your dream wedding venue might be as close as your own back yard – and available for a mere *fee*.

- Local real estate or property management offices – these resources might know of a vacant or rentable property that you could rent for a very nominal price.

- A beautiful barn, farm or ranch can make for a wonderful country setting.

The Typical Venues

Even when you're looking for a good deal, you should still consider some of the typical wedding venues. There are almost always fees involved, but one of these may be better suited to your style and taste. The very best tip for saving money at typical locales is to choose off peak hours/days/seasons. If you do this, you will not only save tons of money, but you will have more date choices!

Typical Wedding Venues Include:

- Place of Worship-you don't even have to belong to one. Many open their venue to anyone. Checkout non-denominational churches too! Many of these can accommodate a reception.

- Restaurants-especially great if they have a spot for the ceremony and then the reception can be moved to the restaurant area.

- Private Clubs.

- Halls-some are there for just such occasions. Don't forget that there are Fire Halls and other Club Halls as well (like Shriners and Optimist Clubs).

- Party Boats/Yachts/Riverboats.

- Hotels-Still wildly popular because everything can take place under one roof, including accommodations for guests.

Solving the "Location" Dilemma by Choosing a Destination Wedding

Choosing a destination wedding can solve a multitude of decision-making dilemmas for you. While some locations aren't cheap, you'll save in other ways such as number of wedding guests, honeymoon expenses (some locations are all-inclusive) and food and entertainment.

Whether you choose a lush tropical island, a medieval castle or a ski resort, you'll have the perfect setting and theme for whatever you want your wedding to be. Some couples choose a destination wedding because family and friends are scattered and the task of getting them all in one place at the same time is daunting.

Others want an intimacy for their wedding that fewer guests and less hassle can provide. They don't want to think about flowers, food, entertainment or any of the other irritations that can plague a wedding.

You can't save money on a destination wedding by paying for all of your guests' travel and accommodation expenses, so be sure you discuss arrangements with possible guests so they'll be able to make an informed decision.

Destination weddings are an ideal venue for freethinking and adventurous couples. If you plan far enough in advance, you should be able to find the perfect exotic location for your wedding for much less than you imagined.

Here are some thoughts for choosing a fun and affordable destination wedding:

- ❀ Resorts, beaches, and other popular "getaways" usually don't require formal attire for activities and have casual activities that everyone can enjoy.

- ❀ If you plan an off-season wedding, you'll be able to get much lower rates. Check with locations you have in mind and consider what you can get that will fit your budget.

- ❀ The number of guests that will travel to your wedding can actually help you get discounts at resorts, airlines and other forms of transportation.

❀ Yacht or cruise ship lines often offer all-inclusive packages for you and your wedding party. All you have to do is show up and leave all the preparations to someone else.

❀ Research through a travel agent. Sometimes they know the best deals available for the increasingly popular destination weddings.

❀ Do your research on the Internet. Helpful advice abounds on a multitude of web sites. They're full of information such as names to contact, what you can expect and even descriptions of an individual experiences.

By thinking outside the norm, you can get the destination wedding of your dreams – within your budget. A little research on your part will go a long way to finding and securing a perfect location for your dream wedding – and you may be able to get it *free!* Think of all the other budget considerations of your wedding where you can put the money you save to better use.

Things to consider when considering a Location:

❀ Do you need any permits?

❀ What's included if anything?

❀ Is the fee tax deductible? (For museums, parks, etc)

❀ How many guests does the venue hold?

❀ Are there time restrictions?

❀ Does the formality match your desired look?

❀ Are there restrictions on decorations?

❀ Is there adequate parking?

❀ Can you use your own vendors or do they have to be approved by venue?

❀ When can you set up for the wedding?

❀ Do they require extra insurance?

❀ Are there enough electrical outlets?

❀ Are there dressing areas available?

- ❖ Are there any restrictions for photography, videography or music?
- ❖ What is the venue's cancellation policy?
- ❖ Can you use your own alcoholic beverages?
- ❖ Do they have a rainy day plan?
- ❖ Do you have to rent items like tables and chairs?
- ❖ What does the overall rental fee include?

How to Choose the Tone and Formality of your Wedding

Setting the tone and formality of your wedding sets the mood and character of the event. The tone can be elegant, romantic, spiritual, a specific theme, casual or festive. Formality comes in by the décor, the attire, the ceremony and perhaps the food.

Deciding the tone and formality totally depends on what you, as a couple, want to focus on. This is where your personalities and the things you have in common can really shine. In other words, if you are an outdoorsy couple, it wouldn't really be fitting to have your wedding in a stuffy venue and vice versa. Decide on tone and formality by keeping in mind what you love, what you love to do and what you both have in common.

Once you decide on Tone and Formality, it will help you decide how to spend money on your wedding, how to choose your wedding elements, like invitations, venues, attire and pretty much everything that goes into your whole day. Remember that your guests will get the tone of the wedding the moment they receive your invitation, so early decisions are needed here. Your guests will rely on this information to help them get ready for your celebration.

Tone and Formality can also be set in the décor you choose, the theme and colors, the lighting, the food, and the ceremony and reception activities.

Wedding Themes are Creative and Fun

There are so many options to choose from. Choosing a theme can make planning easier and save money. Creating themes can be as simple as picking certain colors or as elaborate as your budget allows. Your theme can be included in your engagement party, your shower, and all through the wedding and reception.

Any theme can be done within your budget. It just takes planning and a little help from your family and friends!

Some wedding theme ideas...

❀ Beach/Seaside- Have everyone in the wedding party dressed in white linen or gauze. Or use aqua blues and sea greens. Decorate with seashells and sand. You can add beautiful shells to your cake too! Keep it natural and light.

❀ Eco Friendly/Green- Use less paper. Use local flowers and food. Use less dishes and containers by making things work double duty, like flower seeds as favors! Save energy by celebrating the day at one location. Use recycled items where you can.

❀ Valentines Day or Hearts- Use Red and White everywhere. Doilies rose petals and lace work beautifully with this theme. Use cute Valentine cards as place cards and big Valentine cutouts for decorations.

❀ Paper Wedding- Whether you make some yourself or buy it all. Use paper lanterns, origami birds and paper flowers. Paper butterflies, pinwheels, paper cones, and fans are beautiful too! Even your tablecloths can be paper!

❀ Monochromatic-Use all one color. This makes for an elegant and sometimes modern look. Plus it makes shopping for decorations a snap!

❀ Midsummer- Wear flowers in your hair and keep the wedding party's clothes light. Use sunflowers and daises everywhere. An informal picnic in a garden is fresh and summery and a money saver.

❀ Medieval- Marry in an old church or botanical garden. Rent Medieval costumes for the wedding party. Use dried flowers, nuts and fruits in the décor. Make your own flags, banners, shields, and "family crests". Ladies can wear garlands and flowers in their hair.

❀ Retro- It can be 50s, 60s, 70s…whatever you like! This is a great way to use old family photos, retro music and fun foods!

❀ Black and White- Start with the White bridal gown and Black tuxes or suits and go from there. Carry this theme throughout the entire wedding. Black and White decorations, Black and White cookies, balloons and other decorations! You can also ask the guests to come in creative black and white.

❀ Halloween- This is for the truly adventurous couples. Halloween weddings can be done in a subtle way, or all the way with a full costume party. Let your imagination go wild.

❀ Fall- Picture candy corn in cellophane bags, warm apple cider and apple martinis. Fall is the perfect time to use nature's bounty. Incorporate pumpkins, fall leaves, gourds and nuts. Many of these items are free if you're willing to gather.

❀ Christmas/Holiday- Use the colors of the season. Decorate with Evergreen/Pine boughs and wreaths. Holiday candy works well here. Decorate the tables with fake wrapped presents…very Cheap Chic! Many churches and other houses of worship are already decorated this time of year…take advantage!

❀ Western wedding themes- Think bandanas, arriving on horseback, and barbecue food for the reception. You can even do some square dancing.

❀ Winter White or White on White- Think all white! Use white flowers and silver bows. Wear crystal or rhinestone jewelry. Decorate with floating candles. Use inexpensive tiny white lights. Serve Hot Chocolate, Specialty coffees or Hot Cider.

- Fairytale/Cinderella/Princess wedding themes- Rent costumes for everyone. Use lots of beautiful tulle and ribbon. Decorate with multiples of lit candles. Think Romance!

- Your heritage, culture- Are you Irish? Scottish? Native American? Use your heritage as a base for your theme. Family members and research can help you with making it authentic.

- Victorian wedding themes- Think lots of lace! Use muted shades of pink, purple and creams. Victorian weddings can be indoors or out. Serve tea and sandwiches, or make it coffee and elegant desserts.

The best thing about choosing a theme for your wedding is that it helps make choices easier along the way. You can incorporate as much of the theme elements as you like. You can add your own touches as you go.

Once you choose a theme, you can consider some unique ideas like hiring or asking friends to do things like make cotton candy, juggle, do magic, or "read fortunes". You can also hire belly dancers, a harpist, drum performers, or rodeo performers.

For a twist, you can also combine themes. Just be sure the looks go together. You can do a combo like Paper/Monochromatic, Eco-Friendly/Beach, or Valentines/Paper.

The choices for wedding themes go on and on. Remember to find inspiration around you to tie it all together. Include as much detail involving your theme as budget allows.

Assembling your Wedding Team

Every Bride and Groom needs help in making their wedding day a success. Assembling your team is important. Where budget allows, hire a professional. To save a lot of money, do as much of the work as you (and all of your helpers) can. Don't be afraid to ask for help from family and friends. They want to help!

Here are the basic team members you will need...

- ❀ Officiant- If you belong to a house of worship, you'll likely use the clergy member from there. If you choose a civil ceremony, a judge, justice of the peace, a notary public or court clerk may be used. If you are marrying outside of a house of worship, you may have to use a non-denominational clergy person or civil servant if your clergy does not travel. A few states allow you to use a friend who has been ordained online through the Universal Life Church. Check the laws and rules of your state on who can perform a wedding.

- ❀ Photographer/Videographer- Sometimes you can hire both through the same company. View your potential photographer's previous work. Meet with him/her to discuss your plans and ideas. Ask about packages, the time they spend at your wedding, and how you can cut costs to suit your budget. Hiring a videographer is great if budget allows.

- ❀ Florist-Whether you are hiring a florist or doing the flowers yourself, you still have to gather your resources and shop around.

- ❀ Caterer/Restaurant- The venue you're using will sometimes require that you use their caterer. If you are getting married in an unusual setting, you will have to shop for a caterer/restaurant yourself.

- ❀ Cake Maker- There are lots of choices here...Bakeries, Grocery Stores, Culinary schools, a friend.

- ❀ Music for Ceremony and Reception- Hiring musicians can really add up. Consider mixing recorded music and live music throughout the day to save some money.

- ❀ Invitation company- Many couples choose to do this one themselves. There are tons of resources for discount invitations and kits for DIYers!

- ❀ Transportation- This category has the potential to save you a lot of money. Borrow a relative's cool car, rent discount vans for out of towners, or make a unique entrance on horses, a motorcycle or a rented sedan instead of a limo.

- ❀ Hair stylist and makeup artist- If you have a favorite hair stylist, book them early! Many makeup stores will do your wedding day makeup for FREE!

- ❀ Rentals- Depending on your venue(s), you may need to rent tents, tables, chairs, etc.

General tips for assembling your team:

- ❀ When hiring a professional, do your research and get recommendations from other newlyweds.

- ❀ Ask Questions...How long have they been in business? Are they available on your date and time? How much is the deposit and when is it due? What is the cancellation policy? Can they supply references?

- ❀ Call on 3-5 vendors per category to compare prices.

- ❀ Get an estimate.

- ❀ Negotiate where you can. Some professionals are willing and it doesn't hurt to try!

- ❀ Review all contracts carefully! Be sure your details are all correct like date, time and the services they are offering.

- ❀ Stay in touch with your team members as much as possible or as much as they feel necessary.

- ❀ Keep all estimates, contracts and actual costs in your binder notebook.

- ❀ Does the professional offer any discounts? Like AAA, or from other clubs?

- ❀ Ask about hidden fees, overages, or charges for extras.

- ❀ Are any of the fees/donations tax deductible?

- ❀ If you are using students, a school or amateur, be very clear about your wants and needs and write a formal agreement.

- ❀ If you are using friends or family members, communicate well and express yourself as accurately as you can.

Saving money on your wedding means being organized and tapping into every resource you have. You are probably surrounded by talented people! Ask friends, family members, co-workers, church members and neighbors to help you make your wedding a beautiful day!

A few words about Wedding Planners...If using a planner/coordinator interests you, by all means, check it out. They can help with every aspect of your wedding planning. You have to weigh the pros and cons for you and whether or not it fits your budget. They can often get discounts only offered to them, so shopping for one may help you out.

Accommodations

Depending on other factors in your wedding planning, you may have to make arrangements for you and/or some of your guests. Each guest is responsible for his or her own travel and hotel expenses. Traditionally though, the bride and groom help their guests with getting information about accommodations and airline information too.

A great way to save is to call the hotel of your choice and reserve a block of rooms. Sometimes they offer a room for the bride and groom for free or a discount. If you are having your wedding and/or reception in a hotel, you may find that the hotel will help you out even more! In either case, don't be afraid to negotiate group rates and to also check prices online...sometimes they are even cheaper. Be careful when reserving a block of rooms. Hotels usually make you leave your credit card as a deposit, make you sign a contract and require you to fill a certain number of rooms.

There are a few alternate choices when finding a place for out of town guests to stay. Look for a house or condo in your area that can be rented for a short period of time. You may be able to accommodate more than one family and they can split the expense. Recruit family members to host someone in their home. This is great for all around savings!

What about the bride and groom? You have a few things to consider here...If you are blocking hotel rooms for guests, consider getting a suite for you to use before the wedding and on the wedding night. It's a good idea to start thinking about honeymoon accommodations also, if you will be traveling for a honeymoon.

Here are some additional tips for accommodations:

- ❀ Get to know the seasonal rates in your area. It could mean a huge saving if you book off-season.
- ❀ Check travel websites, even you are only checking room rates.
- ❀ Ask the hotel for additional discounts like AAA, Student, Military, Clubs, and more.
- ❀ If you're staying in a hotel for your wedding night, ask for more time in the room, like early check in or late check out.
- ❀ Try to choose a hotel as close to the wedding site as possible.
- ❀ Offer guests a few choices of hotels with different price points.
- ❀ Find out if the hotel can help your guests with things they may need like handicap accessibility, baby cribs and special meals at their restaurant.
- ❀ Send out of town guests hotel information via your wedding website, a postcard, or a letter. Include direct phone number, name of contact, maps, and directions. Send the info as early as possible (3-6 months ahead if you can).
- ❀ Of course the couple always has the option to stay home for the night before or the night of the wedding. This may be the cheapest and most peaceful option.

Transportation

Wedding transportation can involve many cars and many people. Your first priority is to get the bride and groom where they need to be. Of course, all of your transportation needs must fall within your budget. Traditionally the bride travels with either her maids or her father and mother or all of the above to the wedding site, depending on if she is traveling dressed or is getting dressed at the venue. The groom and groomsmen usually arrange to ride together.

Limousines are the most popular rental for weddings. There are pros and cons to renting limos where budget is concerned. You can certainly rent a limo and use it for a few trips...like to the ceremony then to the reception and then as a bride and groom getaway car. In reality, your guests will not likely see you arrive at the ceremony site and will be on their way to the reception before you're even done with your photos.

It is very easy to eat up a chunk of your budget on transportation. If transportation is not a top priority for you, then consider some cost cutting ideas. This is a great place to perhaps use a person from the wedding party to help organize transportation needs.

Some of the people who may also need transportation are out-of town guests without cars, elderly relatives, parents, siblings and the wedding party. You do not necessarily have to hire cars for all of these folks, but you can certainly help them carpool and drive others. A helper would be perfect here.

Some savings tips for wedding day transportation:

❁ If renting a limo, book in advance to insure there are no last minute charges.

❁ Ask the limo company if you can bring along your own champagne.

❁ Hire a Town Car or other luxury model with driver for a significant price difference.

❁ Rent luxury cars and have your groomsmen escort your VIPs.

❁ Use vintage/retro cars from the 50's, 60's or 70's.

❁ Some classic car club members will rent out their car and will even drive you.

❁ Cut the time of your rental by getting yourself to the ceremony and then using the car for the rest of the day.

❁ Borrow a car from a friend who has a car you like…offer up gas money when you're done.

❁ Color of a limo may make a difference. Sometimes White Limos cost more than black or gray. Check it out.

❁ If you need to move larger groups of guests or wedding attendants, consider renting a 12-passenger van, party bus or an SUV.

❁ Horse and Buggy rides are a romantic alternative for couples. Check your area for availability.

❁ Consider the unusual; you can use snowmobiles, motorcycles, horses, a rowboat, or a snazzy convertible.

❀ Use your own car...have your wedding attendants decorate it! This is a great bargain!

A few more things to remember:

❀ Check references if hiring a service.

❀ Check the company's cancellation policy.

❀ Make sure the potential company is licensed and insured.

❀ Decide 6-9 months ahead if possible. Consider the time of year/ season. It gets tough to rent or hire cars during wedding and prom season. Consider when conventions are in town also.

❀ Check the payment policy of the company you might use.

❀ Read all contracts carefully. What is included? What is not included?

❀ Pay close attention to rate details.

❀ Request the color of car(s) you want.

❀ Ask if the company gives any discounts.

❀ Check the condition of the car(s) that will be used.

❀ Check out the appearance of the driver and ask how he will be dressed the day of the wedding.

❀ Give clear details of the locations of your ceremony and reception.

Working out your wedding transportation details in an organized way can save you a lot of money and headaches and make for a wonderful detail of your wedding. Take your time and solicit help in getting it together.

The Getaway Car

Most couples leave their reception in a decorated getaway car. This is commonly either the groom's or the bride's car. Anyone can be the decorator(s) but it's usually people from the wedding party. Some couples even choose to decorate the car themselves. This can be an inexpensive, fun way to carry on a tradition. You can use streamers, signs, ribbons, banners, cans and bells. Window paint made to use on cars is great too!

Staying Organized with Checklists

We mentioned using a wedding notebook to keep all of your planning organized. It's a good idea to create or print any good checklists you would like to use while planning. You can use checklists for anything ranging from vendor lists to photography shots you'd like. There are many resources for wedding checklists and you can check out our checklists at www.Cheap-Chic-Weddings.com.

Wedding Websites

Starting a Personal Wedding Website is a wonderful idea and can be a very helpful tool. The earlier you set it up, the more you can get out of it. A wedding website is a designated site for a couple to use as a way to communicate all of the news surrounding the wedding plans. The basic idea is to sign up, add your info, collect info and share things like photos and documents.

The Internet is full of wedding website choices and they range in price from free to over $100 a year. The main reason for the price difference is usually the amount you can upload onto the site. Different companies offer the same basic elements, but there are plenty of extras too.

What goes on a Personal Wedding Website?

- ✔ Wedding Details
- ✔ Your Story
- ✔ Wedding Events
- ✔ Accommodations for out of town guests
- ✔ Nearby Restaurants and Attractions
- ✔ Maps and Directions
- ✔ Menus
- ✔ Suggested Attire
- ✔ Wedding Attendant Information
- ✔ Fun activities like Quizzes and Polls

Here are some things that website companies offer:

- ❀ Templates and Backgrounds
- ❀ Customized Pages
- ❀ Checklists
- ❀ Planning Tools
- ❀ Weather Forecasts
- ❀ Wedding Day Countdowns
- ❀ Group Email capability
- ❀ RSVP tracking
- ❀ Registry Links
- ❀ Uploading music, audio or video options

Using a personal wedding website is a great way to save money and save the earth by cutting the use of paper and printed photos. Websites are often used to send out "Save the Dates" and to share digital photos with loved ones! You could eliminate printed maps, directions, and accommodations info as well.

Last and certainly not least, having a website up with current information can also get rid of a lot phone calls. Busy, planning couples need all of the time they can get!

Honeymoon Planning

If you are planning on taking a honeymoon trip, whether it's close or far away, the beginning of wedding planning is the time to plan your honeymoon too. Your honeymoon budget is part of your wedding budget. Saving on any type of honeymoon will involve planning early. Book as early as possible for the best deals.

There are tons of travel deals out there and discounts abound! You must keep in mind that it's not the destination that is most important, it's finding a great place for the two of you to connect and relax and enjoy! Keep in mind that you will be tired after the wedding day and you don't want to overdo it.

Who plans the honeymoon? Traditionally the groom planned the honeymoon, but more and more, couples are planning together.

With some planning and doing a little homework, you can have a trip of a lifetime without spending your life savings or going into debt.

Here are some money saving honeymoon ideas:

* A great general tip is to honeymoon off-season for the area that you are visiting. This could mean big savings!

* Plan a trip that is within an hour or two away from home. Check out nearby resorts, Bed & Breakfasts, local beaches, spas and getaways. We are all guilty of not visiting beautiful spots close to home. Now might be the time! This option saves travel time, obtaining passports, buying airline tickets, etc.

* If you're the outdoors types, plan a camping honeymoon. Most campsites have lots of activities choices like canoeing, fishing and hiking.

* Many companies and clubs offer travel discounts on everything from theme park tickets to flights. Check this out if you belong to AAA, AARP, NRA, Costco, Sam's, BJs Wholesale, Professional Organizations and Unions, or through Credit Card promotions.

Sometimes you can also use student and military IDs for discounts as well.

* Don't forget to use your frequent flier miles and any other rewards programs you participate in.

* You may want to consider a Honeymoon Registry. This is where your guests can gift you through the registry and the money goes for your honeymoon expenses.

❀ Using a travel agent could be a big help time-wise and they are very knowledgeable in finding the right trip for you. Be sure to find one through a recommendation and ask about any fees you may have to pay.

❀ Some couples prefer to shop around and check things out for themselves. There are great online resources, but try to compare prices by calling destinations directly. They will often give you a better rate.

❀ Look into staying at a hostel for a great deal. While it's not for everyone, you can find some with private rooms and bathrooms.

❀ While shopping around and booking your honeymoon, be sure you are aware of any hidden costs and taxes that will be added.

Some Popular Destinations that can be a Good Deal:

❀ Cruises

❀ All-Inclusive Resorts

❀ The Poconos

❀ Disney Vacations

❀ California Wine Country

❀ Niagara Falls

❀ Las Vegas

❀ National Parks-many have great hiking and white water rafting

❀ New Orleans

❀ The Mountains, The Beach, Lakeside

Things to Consider before Traveling

🌸 If you are traveling out of the country, be sure to apply for your passport early and check out any health or vaccine requirements for your destination.

🌸 Account for all expenses when budgeting. Consider airfare, lodging, meals, tips, transportation, souvenirs and any extra activities or excursions.

🌸 Check the weather for where you're headed and for the time you will be there.

🌸 Pack properly. You wouldn't want the extra expense of having to buy something that you could have brought.

🌸 It's a great idea to photocopy your plane tickets; passports and emergency phone numbers and then keep them separate from your wallet, like back at your hotel locked up!

Wedding Attire – For $50 or Less

From designer gown to thrift shop specials, you can find the wedding gown (and other accessories) of your dreams by looking in the right places at the right times. And *do* give yourself plenty of time to shop around.

No matter what your dream wedding dress looks like, you'll find it if you know how to shop. Shopping for wedding apparel and accessories is a true art and a compelling mission. If you know the secrets, there's no need to break the bank or stretch the budget.

Begin by looking through all of the bridal magazines and wedding web sites until you find the gown you've always wanted. David's Bridal even has a web site that lets you "design" your own gown to fit your body with the style you want.

The style of your wedding will also dictate the style of your attire. For example, you wouldn't want to wear an extremely formal gown with a long train if you're going to have a scenic location wedding where there might be thistles – and possibly mud!

There are many ways to find bridal bargains. After you decide what you want the style and tone of your wedding to be you can begin your search.

The wedding attire journey should be fun and enjoyable – and when you look at the wedding photos, you'll want happy memories to pop into your mind about how everything came about.

Here Comes the Bride...

How do you envision your grand entrance? Forget the price tag for a moment. No matter what the cost of the original gown that catches your eye – know that it (or something so similar that you could never tell the difference) can be bought for a fraction of the price.

From an elaborately beaded formal gown to a slinky little number that will look great on a beach, rest assured that you can find the appropriate dress for the right price. Your guests will exclaim that you're a "beautiful bride" and never know if the dress cost $50,000 or $50.00.

To become a smart bridal gown shopper, you'll have to know best places to search. Here are some good ideas to begin:

- ❧ **Bridal shops** – You can find bargains at bridal shops by watching closely for special discounts or sales. If you have unlimited funds, bridal shops might appeal to you because of their vast array of gowns and accessories. Also, many of these shops have been around for years – offering personal service and on-site alterations. Look for little out-of-the-way shops outside of the high priced part of town. Oftentimes, inflated prices are a direct result of high rent.

- ❧ **Outlet shops** – You can find remarkably low prices and a huge selection of everything from bridal gowns to garters. Top designers sometimes turn to these shops -- or have their own -- to place clothing that doesn't sell in regular retail establishments.

- ❖ **Department stores** – Some department stores offer bridal departments – but don't forget to check out the evening dress sections. And, you might also find the perfect wedding dress in the prom dress department. This is a great place to look if you are considering a colored dress.

- ❖ **The Internet** – This may be a little tricky to maneuver, but you can find awesome deals on the 'net. Vera Wang's and Jessica McLintock's are abundantly resurrected on web sites such as eBay – and you can often get them for $50.00 *or less!*

- ❖ These dresses may have never been worn, or only worn once, for a few hours but are being sold at a fraction of the price you could pick it up in a bridal shop.

- ❖ **Vintage Shops** – Antique stores and vintage dress shops can be a treasure trove for exciting collections of formal wear – some, one-of-a-kind. Even if you choose one that needs a little TLC, you'll be sure to pay much less than you would for the same fabric, style and embellishments at a bridal shop.

- ❖ **Rental Shops** – If you're really on a tight wedding clothing budget, this may be the way to go. You can rent traditional dresses and this is a great option if you have a specific themed wedding like Medieval or Halloween. Costumes shops rent beautiful dresses too! Wearing a gown for only a day that costs thousands of dollars, only to wrap it in tissue and leave it in an attic for years might seem like a real waste of money – that you could use more wisely in "another piece of the wedding budget pie."

- ❖ **Trunk Shows** – Don't overlook the amazing deals you can get at designer trunk shows. Sometimes the discount is more than 50% *off!* You may also be able to find attendants' dresses at trunk shows.

- ❖ **Seamstress** – You may have your heart set on a wedding gown so unique that it's impossible to find it on the rack anywhere. This is where a good seamstress can come to your rescue. Interview many in your search – and hire the best your budget can afford.

When you visit his or her work place, notice if it's cluttered or organized, (although the very nature of sewing sometimes looks cluttered). Look carefully at examples of his or her work and when it's time to make the final decision -- **trust your instincts**.

✿ **Thrift Shops** – Check out several thrift stores in your surrounding area. You will be amazed at the selection of wedding gowns to be had. Some have never been worn. For the ones that have, just simply have them dry-cleaned. Be sure and check for any stains so you can let the dry cleaner know. Don't forget you can also have a seamstress make any adjustments for a perfect fit. You can find dresses there for anywhere between $15. to $200. They have all different styles, sizes and shapes. We found a beautiful beaded number for $35! So even with dry cleaning and alterations (if needed) you can still have a dream wedding dress for less.

✿ **Regular Catalogs** – Don't forget regular women's catalogs. Many offer beautiful dresses at great prices because they are not under the "bridal" category. Try Spiegel, Victoria Secret, and J. Crew.

✿ **DIY-** Making your own wedding dress is an ambitious project unless you happen to be a skilled seamstress or are lucky enough to have one in your family. The nice thing about making your own dress or having it made for you, is that not only is it fairly inexpensive but it is also extra sentimental.

HOW TO: Sew a two-piece dress by making a top from your choice of fabric or buying a top. The skirt can be made from about five layers of tulle. Gather, add a waistband and wear a slip underneath. Tulle is very cheap. You don't even have to hem tulle. You can leave it as is or cut around the bottom with scalloped scissors.

✿ **Family Heirlooms:** Wearing your mother's or grandmother's wedding dress is a very nice thing to do.

Informal Wedding Dresses

Informal wedding dresses are becoming more popular. A casual or simple wedding dress can save you a lot of cash. Simplicity in a dress is an up-to-the-minute look. How lucky for us...the ones looking to save some money!

Informal bridal dresses can be modest or short. They can be white, black and white, pink, or any color you want. Plus you have more choices for fabric. You can still have silk, tulle, chiffon or any classic wedding dress material. With an informal dress you can also consider using cotton, denim, linen, gauze or even hemp!

Informal Bridal Dresses are a Great Choice for:

❀ Weddings at home

❀ Beach ceremonies

❀ Eloping to Las Vegas (or anywhere)

❀ Marriages at the courthouse

❀ Second or third marriages

Best of all, informal wedding dresses are perfect if that just fits your style and personality.

Beach Wedding Dresses

Trying to decide between beach wedding dresses? Beach weddings are very popular these days. They are relaxed and romantic and offer a gorgeous backdrop for your ceremony. Informal wedding dresses are still too formal for a beach ceremony. Don't worry; there are so many options when picking a beach bridal dress. A great bonus is the dresses are usually a lot less expensive.

So here are some of the things to consider when choosing a dress for a beach wedding:

- ❀ Short and tea length dresses work best
- ❀ Fabrics like chiffon, georgette, crepe, gauze and linen are perfect for the beach.
- ❀ Hawaiian styled dresses are nice (including the traditional muumuu)
- ❀ Sarongs look fabulous and can be worn in many different ways
- ❀ Don't forget your feet. Bare feet work at a beach wedding but there's also foot jewelry you can wear with or without shoes. This would be a great way to sneak in "something blue".

Plus Size Gowns

There are many plus size wedding dresses available everywhere, but don't forget to look in other departments for formal wear that would be suitable for your wedding. It can be a short dress or mid length as well as a long gown.

Comfort is the most important thing. It will be a long day, so make sure uncomfortable clothing or shoes do not ruin it.

There are many online sites, such as EBay, that offer plus size wedding dresses and other attire. If you decide to order your dress, be sure and ask if it may be returned if it doesn't fit correctly. Have someone else measure you.

Here is how you should measure and other tips:

- ❀ Stand up straight with arms hanging down by your side
- ❀ Measure your bust at the fullest part
- ❀ Measure your waist at your natural waistline
- ❀ Measure your hips at the fullest part
- ❀ When you measure wear the undergarments you'll be using

As far as a flattering style goes, these are things to remember:

* A-line dresses are the most flattering
* Empire waists hide the tummy
* Keep the style of your plus size wedding dress simple with a minimum of decoration. If it's too fussy it makes you look heavier
* Gowns that are too tight also make you look heavier
* A pretty neckline draws attention to your pretty face
* Sleeves should be fitted (no puffy sleeves)
* It is best not to wear a plus size wedding dress that is made from fabric that clings. Fabric that's too shiny isn't good either
* Wear a bra and other undergarments that give really good support
* By all means play up your best feature

By all means shop around a lot to get the best price. You don't have to spend a fortune. If you are lucky enough to have someone sew your plus size wedding dress for you (like mom) that's great because it will be done with a lot of love.

No matter where you're looking for the dress of your dreams, be sure to wear comfortable clothing when you're out and about. Take along a friend or family member (like mom) who will give you true advice rather than exclaiming that every style and color are "gorgeous" on you

Wedding Gown Preservation

Wedding dress preservation is important if you want to enjoy and share your gown for years to come. Your gown should be cleaned as soon as possible. The longer that stains set in the dress the harder it will be to remove them.

For the best possible results, follow the directions on the care label as to either wash it or dry clean it. Be careful of trims like sequins and some beads because some cannot be dry-cleaned. Ask a professional.

Many cleaners specialize in protecting your gown. Ask friends or relatives for a referral.

After the wedding dress preservation is done, it should be packed for storage. You can do it yourself or have the dry cleaner do it.

Here are a few wedding gown storage tips:

- ❀ You can store your dress in a box or on a hanger.

- ❀ Use only acid-free boxes and tissue paper. You can purchase these materials from the Internet, office supply stores or the dry cleaner.

- ❀ Never use plastic to store your dress. It can discolor or destroy your dress.

- ❀ Don't use metal pins or clips...they can rust.

- ❀ Store the dress in a cool, dry place.

Accessory Bargains Galore!

After the gown is chosen, get ready to accessorize. Accessories add a finishing touch. This is an area where scads of money can be saved, if you know what you're doing. In the past few years, there's been a do-it-yourself craze among brides – and the craft stores have profited.

The first thing to consider when choosing your bridal headpiece is your hairstyle. Once you decide on your look, (i.e. up-do, down and natural, etc.) try on every veil or headpiece you can get your hands on. Experiment and then try on more. Do this of course with your hair somewhat in your chosen style.

Your bridal headpiece should match the style of your wedding. It doesn't have to match the style of your dress but it should be appropriate (i.e. a long veil for a formal church wedding or a wreath headband for a garden wedding, etc.).

There are lots of different styles of headpieces to top off your look:

1. Tiaras
2. Back Pieces
3. Barrettes or Combs
4. Wreath of Flowers
5. Hats
6. Single flower
7. Brooch or Jewelry
8. Veils

Below are some wedding day accessories that you may need – and, some ways that you can avoid exorbitant prices.

❀ **Veil or Headpiece:** Kits offering veil and headpiece items for under $25.00 can be found in almost any craft store. You can fashion the contents into a high quality, one-of-a kind item that you can truly be proud of – after all, you made it yourself!

A great way to save cash on your wedding veil is to make your own. Don't be afraid-it's pretty simple. Going to a bridal store and buying a wedding veil could cost anywhere from $50 to $300 plus. If you make a bridal veil from materials purchased at the craft store you could save up to $200 bucks or so.

1. You can buy veiling which has already been cut and gathered and ready to attach to a headpiece.
2. If you or someone you know is a seamstress you can purchase a pattern.
3. They even have bridal veil kits at fabric stores. The kits are pretty inexpensive and come with the instructions and all the materials you need.
4. A simple yet elegant idea is to attach fresh flowers to a plastic comb.
5. Another beautiful option is to make a floral headband. This is super easy!

HOW TO:

All you need is:

1. White headband
2. One stem silk hydrangeas
3. One stem silk sweat peas

Remove flowers from stems.
Start at the top of headband, working down each side, glue flowers to band.
Alternate sweet peas with hydrangeas.
We love this idea because you could do your headpiece, your bridesmaid's and flower girl's all for a few bucks.

If you're planning to use hair décor for your headpiece, look at the costume jewelry counters in department stores. Duplicates of high-priced tiaras and other items are readily available for a fraction of the cost.

Flowers in your hair add an exotic touch without being too expensive. Your hairdresser can easily weave them into your locks the morning of your wedding or you can pin them in yourself. Flowers are especially great for a beach wedding.

Remember to keep your veil or headpiece in line with the style of your wedding dress. If your dress is informal, a simple hat or garland of flowers might be a stunning addition. Have fun creating your own wedding headpiece for your special day.

❀ **Lingerie:** You may not be able to skimp on some of these items – especially if you chose a wedding dress that depends on the undergarments to fit properly. For example, if you're wearing a strapless gown, the appropriate bra will be important to the fit of the gown.

Don't assume that you have to buy your lingerie at the same place you bought your dress.

Shop around in chain stores or look in lingerie catalogs for great styles and prices that won't put your budget into shock.

✿ **Shoes:** There's only one big DON'T here – don't purchase shoes that hurt your feet! No matter how great they match your dress, you'll be miserable if you're in pain all day or evening. Shoes should be stylish and comfortable.

A plain, white shoe from a discount shoe store is perfectly okay and will be kind to your budget. Some brides are choosing ballet slippers – or even going barefoot if the ceremony is held on the beach. Whatever style you choose, go with a lower, wider heel. You'll be glad you did when the dancing begins or if you're outdoors (sharper heels tend to sink into the ground).

A few things to remember about wedding day shoes:

1. Don't wait until the last minute to buy them.
2. Get them at the same time you get your dress. You can match your wedding shoes to the style of your dress and also have time to break them in.
3. Wear them about an hour each day one week before the wedding.
4. Apply some non-slip pads or rough them up on concrete so there's so slipping or sliding on the wedding day.
5. If you are wearing a long dress your shoes won't even be noticed. Low heel shoes are great to wear (comfortable).
6. Don't forget to look online for discount wedding shoes. But order in plenty of time in case they don't fit and you have to return them.
7. For a beach wedding you can even wear fancy flip-flops or slip a simple narrow ribbon under your big toe, then cross it over the toe and bring it around your ankle and tie a bow.
8. If you're on a tight budget, don't choose a shoe from a bridal salon. They tend to be overpriced and totally unnecessary. After all, you'll probably only wear them once.
9. Pastel wedding shoes are very stylish now to wear with your white dress. It would be great to wear blue ones for your "something blue".

10. Another inexpensive way to go is to buy shoes you can wear after your wedding. For example, you could wear a pair of silver, gold, velvet or even pink leather sandals. They would be beautiful wedding shoes and can be worn later with a dressy outfit or even jeans!

There are plenty of lavishly embellished bride shoes on the market. Most are very expensive, however you can embellish a plain pair of shoes or flip-flops yourself.

HOW TO:

Use fabric glue to attach anything you'd like to a fabric shoe. You could use beads, sequins, rhinestones, pearls, flowers, lace or a particularly meaningful charm.

Stitching them on is an alternative method for attachment. Or just add a few stitches after gluing for security.

Look in wedding magazines for designer shoes to get ideas for decorating your shoes.

❖ **Jewelry:** This accessory can be perfect for the "something borrowed" category of accessories. If you have a good friend or relative who has the perfect jewelry accessory for your dress, don't be too shy to ask.

If you're adamant to pick out your own jewelry, shop at discount stores, department stores, catalogs or the Internet to save big.

❖ **Gloves, Wraps and Other Niceties** – These accessories are hardly ones that will become sentimental to you or that you should spend lots of money on to get exactly what you want.

Depending on the style of your dress, you may need gloves to wear during the ceremony, but after the important first dances at the reception you can take them off or leave them on, as you choose.

A wrap may be necessary if you're having an evening wedding, or if the ceremony or reception will be held outdoors.

Handbags and hosiery will take an extremely small chunk of the pie – especially if you shop for sales. Usually, the more simple the handbag, the more it will complement your dress.

A garter is another great way to incorporate the "something blue" into your attire. Inexpensive garters are easy to be had. Since the garter will be tossed away…no need to spend a lot of money on it.

As with all other wedding accessories, try to shop wisely and get the most bang for the buck by shopping discount stores, fabric shops, catalogs or the Internet.

If you give yourself plenty of time, you should have no problem finding bridal accessory bargains galore!

Attendants Attire – Making a Penny-Wise Decision

Bridesmaids:
You won't be doing your bridesmaids any favors by choosing a dress style that's so unflattering they'll toss it in the "Goodwill" bin the day after the wedding.

Research bridal attendants' dresses in bridal magazines to get an idea of what choices will meet your approval. You'll have a good idea of styles, colors and prices before you begin to shop.

If you're having an informal wedding, the bridesmaids' dresses don't have to match perfectly in style or even color. As long as the style and color of the dresses are coordinated within a "collection," you'll have a unified look.

Opting for formal wedding attire might be a bit more involved, but keep in mind that even if you're wearing a long, formal gown – your bridesmaids don't have to. As long as colors and styles are coordinated, the look will be set.

Since the bridesmaids will be paying for their own dresses, show special consideration for their body types and budget. No style of dress looks great on everyone, and the same goes for color.

Just as you're shopping for bargain deals for accessories in order to make your budget stretch as far as possible, help your bridesmaids to make similar decisions. For example, don't insist that all of their shoes match. Coordinating the colors will work just fine.

Be sure to go with at least one of your attendants when choosing an appropriate dress and accessories. Department stores will more than likely have coordinating dresses in all your bridesmaids' sizes. Don't be embarrassed to ask for a special discount if you're purchasing them all at one place.

You may find bridesmaid dress bargains in places like catalogues; Victoria Secret, J.Crew or Spiegel.

Flower Girls:

Remember the flower girl, too. Communion and Easter dresses are perfect choices for flower girls. Look for "after the ceremony" or after Easter sales on these dresses for great bargains.

For the little one's headpiece, try Communion departments or choose real or artificial flowers to create a garland for her head. Shoes and gloves for little girls can be found in any discount store for a nominal charge

A flower girl basket and other darling accessories complete the flower girl's look. The basket usually holds flower petals, either real or silk or even potpourri to match the wedding colors. A flower girl basket can run anywhere from $20.00 to $85.00! You can save so much by making a basket yourself.

HOW TO - Flower Girl Basket

Take a small white basket and glue silk hydrangeas, roses or daisies all over the basket (the more the better) until it's completely covered. Wrap the handle with ribbon. You can also tie ribbon at the bottom of the handle and let ends dangle.

For a warm weather wedding, take a small wicker basket and just hot glue a few silk flowers (like daisies) on either side of the handle.

For a cooler weather wedding, cover the basket in satin and embellish with flowers or ribbon.

Don't Forget the Guys

In all the hullabaloo, to choose just the right bride and bridesmaids' dresses, the guys' attire can often be overlooked. After all, they almost always rent their clothing from a formal wear shop.

Special consideration should be given as to coordinating the men's clothing with the bride and her attendants. They should be uniform in their style and color so that group portraits don't look out of sync.

Men don't need tuxedos if your wedding is informal. A dressy suit or other attire will do nicely. Even khaki pants combined with a navy blazer could look great at an informal wedding.

If the groom – or groomsmen often have occasion to wear a tuxedo, it may prove more economical to buy rather than rent. Compare various formalwear shops to get the best prices on renting or purchasing tuxedos. Also, *ask about discounts* if you're renting or purchasing several suits.

Saving money on rentals is not impossible:

- ✿ Take a look on the Internet before heading to the stores. You will likely find a lot of useful coupons, deals or in-store bargains.

- ✿ Don't be afraid to ask for something that another retailer is offering. Many stores offer the groom a free rental with the rental of the rest of the tuxedos.

- ✿ Visit Wedding shows and Expos to meet with vendors in the business. You might be able to do one-stop shopping!

- ✿ Some department and men's fashion stores still do tuxes. Check them out too.

Don't forget these few important tips that may save time and money later...

❀ Ask when your tuxes will be available.

❀ Make sure to designate a pick-up person AND a back up.

❀ Ask if the company has a return or cancellation policy.

❀ Check your order BEFORE the guys leave the tux shop. Check shoes and accessories too!

❀ Be sure to find out about any deposit, balance dues, and when they are to be paid.

❀ Ask exactly when the tuxedos are to be returned.

Whatever your final decision, be sure to urge your groomsmen to check that everything ordered from a formal wear shop (including the correct sizes) is included in the package **before** the wedding day to avoid last minute disasters.

No matter if your wedding is formal or informal – church or faraway resort – you'll want your wedding party to look fresh and unique. It's also important for the photo and video results if the colors and styles mesh.

Given enough time and using our handy tips, you should be able to have the look you want without causing shockwaves through your budget plan.

Imagine...Inexpensive Invitations

Your wedding invitations are a reflection of you as a couple and what your wedding will be like. Invitations are the first clue to your guests as to what the tone and formality of your wedding will be like. Communicating your wedding plans has never been easier with all the ways and means you have at our disposal today. With so many choices, there are many ways to save money while getting invitations you love.

Invitations can get quite costly, especially when considering add-ons that are offered like calligraphy, embossing and extra postage. How you pick and choose the elements of your invitations and other stationery can make or break your budget. Do your homework and think carefully when shopping for invitations whether you buy them through a stationer or do them yourself.

Invitations should be mailed about 6 weeks before the wedding. Be sure to allow enough time to order your invites with time to spare for addressing the envelopes.

Save the Date Notices

Do you really need save the date notices? You might not. Cutting out these mail-outs could save you money. Save the date cards are, of course, a personal preference. They are a good idea if you are planning on a long engagement or your wedding is planned for a special time, like a holiday weekend.

Save the Date Ideas that save you money:

- ✿ Email friends and family to save the date or use and electronic invitation site online.

- ✿ If you have signed up for a wedding website, this is a great place to announce the date. You just have to be organized with your email list to pull this off.

- ✿ Send cute or nostalgic postcards with the wedding date. Make your own or buy local tourist type postcards or cards from a local museum or attraction.

- ✿ Take a photo of the two of you holding a sign with the info and have it copied at home or the drugstore and mail out. You can also create a photo card at the drugstore like those used for holiday cards.

- ✿ There are some great photo postcards available online. They offer beautiful design choices and easy instructions.

- ✿ Have magnets printed with your save the date information.

- ✿ DIY...Buy business card stationery at your local office supply store and print your own using software.

- ✿ If your guest list is manageable, call each guest/couple and let them know when the wedding will take place.

Stationers and Print Shops

There are plenty of retail choices when it comes to buying invitations and other wedding stationery. Not only are they sold in stationery shops and wedding boutiques, but they can also be found at office supply stores, print shops, catalogs, warehouse stores, and the Internet. If you are not the do-it-yourself type, this may be the right choice for you. There are definite benefits to using an expert.

Cost cutting ideas when shopping retail:

- ❀ Do your homework, shop around and know your budget. Prices can vary a lot between retailers and the Internet.

- ❀ Know your paper...choose a lesser grade/weight of paper to save some bucks.

- ❀ Cut some paper out when ordering. Use one envelope instead of two and drop things like Reception Cards and tissue inserts. It's OK to print ceremony and reception information on your invitation.

- ❀ Leave out other inserts. Maps and directions can be announced on your website or handed out at the ceremony if your reception is at another location. The same goes for Accommodation Cards, Transportation Cards, etc. If you can do without, than by all means do.

- ❀ Plan ahead and be ready with what you want. Many retailers will offer you a package deal. The discounts apply when you order everything at once. Just be careful you are not buying items that you don't need.

- ❀ Shy away from expensive extras at the stationers. Add-ons, borders, liners, and fancy designs cost more money.

- ❀ The Internet can be a great resource. Be careful and comparison shop. It wouldn't hurt to get a recommendation from a friend.

- ❀ Use a postcard as your RSVP card. The postage is cheaper!

- ❀ Always order extra envelopes and invitations. It helps to be prepared for mistakes and you may avoid last minute printing charges!

- ❀ Consider printing in one color only. Usually more colors equal more money.

- ❀ Do a combination of professional printing and DIY. Once your invites are printed, embellish them yourself using ribbon or vellum or stationery seals.

- ❀ When ordering from an online invitation company, be sure to use secure ordering, compare prices and ask friends for recommendations.

Invitation Printing Techniques

Professional printers offer some choices when it comes to printing styles. Prices can range drastically, so be sure to price check the different styles.

Engraving: This is the most traditional and most expensive type of printing. It is a formal style with raised lettering and denting on the back of the print

Thermography: This process gives a raised letter effect but is less costly than engraving.

Letterpress: This trendy style is a handcrafted, artsy type of printing using old world presses to create invites. Letterpress has a rustic look.

Offset and Digital: These choices display a flat printed style and are the cheapest choices in professional printing.

Design

Traditionally, wedding invitations have been white or off white with black print. While this is still considered to be pretty and classically styled, there are tons more choices when it comes to design.

Choosing the design of your invitations is where the bride and groom's personalities can shine. The design also sets the tone of your wedding and gives guests an idea of what your wedding will be like.

If you are having your invites printed professionally, they generally have someone on hand to help with custom design or help in choosing a design from catalogs. Invitations range anywhere from traditional/formal to modern and casual. Colors and Font choices are endless too.

Wedding invitations should include...

The Bride and Groom's full names

Wedding Date and Day of the week

The time of the wedding

Ceremony location including address

Reception location including address
(if different from ceremony)

All four parents names

RSVP information

It is very important to be exact on spelling and addresses here!

Wedding invitations come in different shapes and folds. An invitation can be a single card, a one-fold card or two-fold card. Know ahead of time that square invitations and odd shaped invitations can require extra postage.

Wording

There are as many ways to word your invitations, as there are styles to choose from. Wording can be traditional with formality, modern and casual or anything in between. This is another way to set the tone for your wedding. Formal wording with a fancy font tells your guests that you are having a traditional wedding while casual wording and font says you are having a modern or casual affair.

We suggest you do a little research and find the wording that works best for you as a couple. If you are having your invitations printed, they can help you with proper wording. If you're making your own invitations, there are tons of resources online to help you decide. A general rule of thumb and proper etiquette dictates that the person or people hosting the wedding get mentioned first on the invitation. If it's more that one set of parents hosting and/or the bride and groom, then you include all.

This is what a typical traditional invitation would look like...

Mr. and Mrs. John Smith
Request the honor of your presence
At the marriage of their daughter
Mary Elizabeth Smith
To
Michael David Jones

Saturday, the Eleventh of June
Two Thousand and Eleven
At Five O'clock in the Evening

Hometown Country Club
123 Country Club Lane
Boca Raton, FL
Reception to Follow

Cocktail Attire

A more casual approach to wording could look like this...

Mary Elizabeth Smith
&
Michael David Jones
request the pleasure of your company
at their marriage

Saturday, June 11, 2011
At 5:00 PM

Hometown Country Club
123 Country Club Lane
Boca Raton, FL

Reception to Follow

Cocktail Attire

Doing It Yourself

Making your wedding invitations may be something for you to consider. With good planning and a little know-how you could save a lot of money by making your invitations. Take into consideration the time it will take, your skill level, your design sense and how much help you can get from others.

Many stores, including craft stores, stationery stores, discount department stores and office supply stores, now offer wedding invitation kits and all types of stationery to use. Kits are also sold on the Internet as well.

Kits are generally packaged in bundles of 25 or 50 and will include invitations, invitation envelopes, RSVP cards, and RSVP envelopes. Some kits may include labels, seals and/or thank you notes, but generally these are sold separately.

You can use regular stationery or cards for invitations as well. Don't shy away from pretty paper just because it's not labeled as "wedding" invitations. The big secret here is to make sure that you have the right size envelopes for the size stationery you want to use. Shop for the envelopes first then work your way in…

Here are some great Do-it-Yourself Invitation tips:

- ❀ Window shop at invitation stores for inspiration.
- ❀ Use a design computer program with pre-made templates.
- ❀ Use a laser printer or the best quality printer available to you.
- ❀ Ask an artistic friend to help you design your invitations.
- ❀ Be careful when using images. Sometimes the images become blurry when blown up or changed.
- ❀ Take a calligraphy class if you want to address your envelopes with beautiful style. Caution: this works best for addressing a small amount of invites.
- ❀ While practicing your invitation printing, use plain paper!
- ❀ Use .5 margins.
- ❀ Browse the Internet for design ideas and templates.
- ❀ If you're looking for specific paper colors, look at card stock and colored papers.

❀ Embellish your invitations with ribbon, bows, vellum overlays and photos.

❀ Consider using drawings, icons or monograms for a unique look. Carry the design over to all of your stationery and even favors and decorations!

❀ Use a plain hole-punch, then weave ribbon through for a professional look.

❀ Use decorative scissors or funky hole-punches to spice up your cards.

❀ Use a photo lab (or your local pharmacy) to make photo invites (a la holiday cards)!

❀ If you're having a very small wedding, consider hand writing your invitations.

❀ Decorative seals or special stickers add a nice touch to your envelopes!

❀ Create your design at home then have it duplicated at a print shop or office supply store.

❀ A great DIY trick is stay consistent throughout your wedding stationery. It looks more professional when you use the same design/logos/photos/fonts on everything from invitations to programs.

❀ Make 10-25 extra invitations.

❀ Be sure to keep a few for yourself. You might want to pass them to the kids!

❀ Recruit help for when you are ready to stuff and address your invitations.

❀ Best tip: Proofread, Proofread, and then proofread again. Ask someone else to look your work over before you print!

A Few Words on Invitation Etiquette

Good Etiquette is the same as common sense! It includes inclusion and being kind. It also includes general respect for others. Here are a few tips on invitation etiquette:

- ❀ Only use periods after a title like Mr. and Mrs. And Ms.

- ❀ Only use commas when writing out dates.

- ❀ Be sure you send an invitation to your Officiant/Clergy and their spouse.

- ❀ It is considered impolite to write "No children". Instead, be sure to only write those persons invited on the inner envelope. It is proper to address children questions in person/on the phone.

- ❀ Inner envelopes are addressed with exact names of invitees. For example, John and Mary Smith with Susie Smith listed on the second line for minors. Children 18 and older should receive their own invitation.

- ❀ It is perfectly acceptable to write "Mr. Robert Jackson and Guest" for unmarried guests.

- ❀ Be sure to write Military titles on inner and outer envelopes when it applies.

- ❀ The only abbreviations you should use are Mr., Mrs., Ms., Dr. and Jr. when addressing invites.

- ❀ It is considered passé to write only the husband's name when addressing a couple. Either write Mr. and Mrs. Jones, or Mr. and Mrs. William and Mary Jones.

- ❀ You can leave off Mr. and Mrs. on invitations. Just use first and last names.

- ❀ On formal invitations, write out the times and dates.

- ❀ On your RSVP cards, allow about 30 days between the return date and the wedding date.

- ❀ Do not include Registry information on your invitation. You can include this information on your wedding website or spread the word through friends and family.

✿ The general rule on listing names on the invitation is that the person or couple hosting goes first on the invitation. The Bride's parent's names go first then the Groom's parents. If you have divorced and/or remarried parents then the Bride's mother and her spouse go first, then the Bride's father and spouse and so on.

Calligraphy

Calligraphy is an ancient art of beautiful handwriting using decorative strokes with special pens and ink. Calligraphy used on wedding invitations and/or envelopes is considered formal and elegant. Hiring a professional calligrapher can be quite expensive.

It is possible to learn calligraphy yourself and incorporate the look on your invitations. If you're not ambitious enough to make all of your invitations in this style, consider using it only to address your invitations or to draw a monogram only on your invites or envelopes.

Calligraphy classes are available in some areas and you can certainly learn from many calligraphy websites. There are books available on the subject as well. If you are interested in teaching yourself, consider buying a do it yourself book for children.

While there are some beautiful pens and inks made just for calligraphy there are also some great products available for the novice. A few companies make chiseled calligraphic markers and pens geared toward the crafter.

You can get the "look" of calligraphy simply by choosing a calligraphy style font when printing your wedding stationery. Great places to use calligraphy are invites, place cards, programs and favors.

Alternatives to Traditional Invitations:

More and more, couples are making wedding choices that don't always fall under the "traditional" category. If you are not into traditional invites or want to save even more money there are a few alternatives.

Consider using postcard invitations! They are not for everybody, but can certainly work, especially for casual and non-formal weddings. Just be sure to set up a way for folks to RSVP...like via phone or email. Postcards mean less postage!

Use an E-vite site on the Internet to invite your guests. This is a low to no cost alternative to mailing invitations!

Sending an invitation via email is definitely not traditional, but can be used, especially if it's a spur of the moment event.

Are you into photos? Send a photo invitation! Use a website like Shutterfly.com or have invites printed at your local photo processor. Again, be sure to make it easy for people to respond.

Going Green!

If reducing your impact on the environment is important to you, then you might want to go green when it comes to wedding invitations and stationery. You can help save trees, water, energy and money!

The two biggest ways to be eco-friendly in this area is to reduce the amount of paper you use and/or use recycled and alternative products. You can have beautiful invitations and sentiments and of course, buying less paper can mean big savings!

Reducing the use of paper:

- ❀ Cut out paper altogether...email invites and save the dates, call your guests with invitations, video tape yourself and send links to your YouTube invite, or set up a Personal Wedding Website with all of your information!

- ❀ Reduce some of the paper...If you'd like to have paper invitations, have guests call in their RSVPs or email back to you. This reduces the amount of paper inserts in your invitation.

- ❀ Use postcards where possible.

- ❀ Use Electronic Invitations online where you can.

Choose your materials carefully:

- ✿ Use the highest percentage recycled paper that you can... preferably 100%.

- ✿ If you are making invitations and stationery, use craft items you have on hand.

- ✿ Ask your print professional to use vegetable-based or soy ink.

- ✿ Online shopping will reveal that many vendors offer environmentally friendly products for weddings.

- ✿ Look for tree-free paper like stationery made from hemp, cotton, flax, bamboo and other fibers.

Double Duty Ideas:

- ✿ Use your favors as place cards. Write on your favors directly.

- ✿ Use seed embedded paper for place cards and programs. Guest can plant them in the ground later for pretty flowers.

- ✿ If you must use printed maps, use the other side for more info, like your rainy day plan.

Postage

If you are mailing invitations, you can count on the fact that you will have to buy postage. Invitations are mailed First Class by the Postal Service. It is a good idea to take a finished/stuffed invitation to the post office to find out what the postage will be. There are specific guidelines when mailing letters and invitations are often larger and heavier than a regular letter.

Don't forget to buy postage for your RSVP envelopes or postcards while purchasing your other postage. Remember that postal rates might be different for odd shaped or oversized envelopes as well.

USPS Guidelines for first class postage:

Dimensions

> Rectangular.

> At least 3 ½ inches high by 5 inches long by .007 inches thick.

> No more than 6 1/8 inches high by 11 ½ inches long by ¼ inch thick.

> Maximum weight is 3.5 ounces.

> Letters considered non-machinable are subject to additional charges.

> Length is the dimension parallel to the address.

Post Cards

> Minimum size of 3 ½ inches high by 5 inches long by .007 inches thick.

> Maximum size of 4 ¼ inches high by 6 inches long.

> Additional postage is required for larger postcards.

The post office usually offers "Love" stamps or wedding stamps for sale for letters that are One ounce or less and letters that are Two ounces or less. If you have trouble finding these at your local post office, you can purchase them online at www.usps.com.

Specialty postage stamps are available at many online sites. There are custom ones, photo stamps and really every theme and color you can imagine. Specialty stamps cost more than standard stamps, so be aware and shop accordingly. These sites usually discount for larger purchases.

If vintage is your thing and you want to use vintage stamps, it's perfectly fine, just remember that these stamps have lesser value than current stamps and you will have to multiple stamps on each envelope.

Worried about your invitations going through machines at the post office? You can pay an extra fee to have yours "hand cancelled".

There are only so many ways to save on postage and the only way to avoid it altogether is to hand deliver as many invitations as possible. Of course, this is not traditional and you should only do this where you feel comfortable.

A Few More Invitation Tips:

- ❀ We can't say it enough...Proof Proof Proof...Read over everything several times and ask others to help you proofread everything for correct address and spelling!

- ❀ Allow 2-6 weeks for printing your invitations, about 1-2 weeks to address and stuff your invitations, and send about 6 weeks ahead of your wedding.

- ❀ Don't go it alone...recruit help when you are ready to put your invitations together and address them!

- ❀ Personal Wedding Websites can be a great help and can also eliminate the need for so much paper. Some are offered for free or a small cost. You can use your site to share information like directions, maps, accommodations, rainy day plans, rehearsal dinner plans, registry info, RSVP information, menus and even photos!

Thank You Cards

Writing thank you notes, is not only a nice thing, it's mandatory! That's right...no shortcuts here...you must send a hand written note, from you, for every gift you receive. It's also appropriate to send thank you notes to those who have hosted parties for you, to your parents and family members who have contributed and your attendants!

It is perfectly fine to use store bought boxed cards. You do not have to buy fancy custom thank you cards. The most important thing is that you send thanks and that you do so as soon as possible after you receive the gift or help or service. We suggest you send thank you cards within a few weeks of getting gifts.

It's a great idea to get organized and keep a running list of gifts as you get them, with the names and info of the giver and whether or not you have sent a thank you.

Other Stationery, Paper and Etc.

The paper and printed items don't stop at just invitations. You may find that you need or want some of these stationery items. Remember that if you are Doing It Yourself, you can customize these items and have a theme or color scheme running throughout.

- ✿ Announcements-letting everyone know you're engaged
- ✿ Save the date cards
- ✿ Pre wedding party invitations-like showers and bachelorette parties
- ✿ Programs-lets people know what's happening on the wedding day
- ✿ Rehearsal dinner invitations
- ✿ Location maps and directions
- ✿ Place cards/Seating cards-Reception seating
- ✿ Table number cards
- ✿ Menus
- ✿ Personal stationery
- ✿ Guest Book
- ✿ Some couples choose to enclose specific cards in their invitations like the map, rainy day plan, pew cards, wedding website info.

Fun Ways to Save Money on Pre-Wedding Parties

Pre-wedding parties are fun times that lead up to your big day. It's when you're good friends and your family join together to start the celebration of your upcoming marriage. You can have great parties and create lasting memories without spending a fortune.

The Parties Are:

- ❀ The Engagement party
- ❀ The Bridal Shower
- ❀ The Bachelor Party

- ❧ The Bachelorette Party
- ❧ The Rehearsal Dinner

The Engagement Party is not so popular anymore, but if you want to have one to make the announcement of your upcoming wedding by all means do. However if everybody already knows that you are engaged just skip this party and save even more money.

Don't invite anyone that won't be invited to the wedding. That would be a big NO NO.

A cocktail party with simple hors d'oeuvres would be fine. To save money, serve wine and beer only. This would be a great way to break the news to your friends. A lot of your very closest friends will probably already know but that's o.k. After the party everyone will know.

The Bridal Shower is and always will be a very popular party. The budget should be decided on at the beginning. With the help of friends and family expenses can be cut but the quality of the party will still be great.

Up until now it has been customary for the maid-of –honor to host the shower. Times have changed. Now it is acceptable for a friend or even a family member to have the party.

The hostess should consult with the bride on the date of the shower, the time, the theme and anything else that she wants.

Men are invited to some showers but you don't have to do that if the bride doesn't want it. It would be more expensive plus if you wanted to have a lingerie party, for example, then it wouldn't be cool to invite them.

One of the best places to hold the shower is at the hostess' home. It is not only a more friendly setting but it is a big money saver. It's free to use. You could have the shower at the home of the bride's mother if the maid of honor can't have it at her home.

Wedding showers should be held one to two months before the wedding. The invitations are sent out two to four weeks before the shower. The invitations include the RSVP with a request that they be sent back one to two weeks before the shower.

Ask your bridesmaids and family members to help you with addressing the invitations.

The invitations bought at the store are really not very expensive but you can pay even less by hand-making them or printing them on your computer.

The day of the shower should be very organized. Having a plan for the general idea of the order of the activities is important.

- ❀ Set out hors d'oeuvres and drinks before guests arrive.
- ❀ Introduce each guest once they are all there.
- ❀ Play any games at this point to break the ice.
- ❀ Everyone can help themselves to the drinks and food
- ❀ Enjoy cake or dessert and let bride-to-be open her gifts!

After everyone has arrived introduce each one. Now it's time to play some games and get the party going. Here are some that are a lot of fun.

- ❀ **The Bridal Gown** Game is by far one of the most popular game around and that is because it is so much fun. The hostess furnishes several rolls of toilet paper and guests are broken up into teams. Each team chooses a model and the teams design wedding gowns using ONLY toilet paper wrapped around the model. The bride chooses the winner. This is definitely a favorite game.

- ❀ **Bride Bingo** can be purchased inexpensively at party stores or you can make your own on your computer.

- ❀ **Word Scramble** is fast and fun. The hostess compiles 12-15 words having to do with weddings. Using your computer create a document listing each word scrambled. Guests will try to unscramble the words in 5 minutes. The person with the most correct answers wins a prize.

- ❀ **Clothespins Game** is another that is particularly liked. The hostess gives a clothespin or mini-clothespin to each guest. She tells everyone a specific word that is off limits (like the grooms name or the word wedding). The game begins when everyone has arrived. Every time someone says the forbidden word, the person that catches her, gets her pin. The person with the most pins at the end of the game wins a prize.

- ❀ **Bride Trivia Game** tells who knows the most about the bride or at least who remembers the most. The hostess gets facts about the bride before the shower. Use questions like favorite color, favorite food, and where the couple met, etc. 20 questions are enough. The hostess makes a question sheet on the computer and gives it to the guests. The person that has the most correct answers after a set amount of time wins a prize.

- ❀ **Name Game.** Prepare game sheets with the bride and grooms names on the top of the sheet. The person that makes the most words using the letters of their names wins a prize.

Wedding shower games are inexpensive and can be great fun. There are several websites on the Internet where you can download FREE bridal shower games. Take advantage of these and have fun.

Prizes for the games can be purchased inexpensively at a party store. You can purchase some cute things for your hair, inexpensive jewelry, small makeup bags, headbands and the list goes on and on. These things can be found at stores like Target, K-mart or Wal-Mart and others. You may find something at the craft store that you can whip up fast.

Now it's time to eat and here are some ideas for that. Let's keep the budget in mind. That doesn't mean that it won't be good. It certainly can be excellent.

The best way to save money on the food is to make it yourself with the help of friends and family. Don't be shy about enlisting others to help you.

Traditionally women enjoy light food like finger foods including finger sandwiches and gelatin salad (don't eat the gelatin salad with your fingers.), just kidding. These foods are also light on the budget. Of course you may have some warm food if you like, just keep it simple. You can ask others that have special dishes they make to contribute their cooking talents. You don't have to do that either. Here are some other ideas.

If the shower is at an odd time of day just serve hors d'oeuvres or finger foods only. Use inexpensive trays from the local deli or supermarket or make them yourself (that is better on the budget). Choices are enormous. Use cheese and crackers, mini meatballs, cut vegetables and dip, chips and dip, deli meat platters with bread. That is only the beginning of ideas. Check your cookbooks and magazines and don't forget, you'll have some great ideas yourself.

Dessert and coffee is an elegant choice if the party is after dinnertime. Make a few homemade decadent desserts and serve them with gourmet coffee and flavored creams.

Wine and cheese can also be served at an afternoon or after dinner shower. Make sure to offer something to the teetotalers. Buy the wine and cheese to fit your personal budget.

Instead of serving wine make a punch with wine in it. That would be a lot less expensive than just wine. You could have some punch without the wine for the people that don't drink it. There are lots of recipes for it. Find them on line or in cookbooks.

A lunch buffet can be inexpensive if you plan ahead. Serve attractive sandwiches and salads. What they say is true; presentation is everything. Make the buffet decorative, fun and appetizing. Serve the food at different levels to add interest.

Bridal food choices go on and on. Make menu decisions based on your comfort level. Consider theme, locale and budget.

When the meal starts to wind down, start the bride with opening the gifts. Make sure someone writes down each gift and whom it's from.

As people leave and say their goodbyes, the hostess may want to hand out favors. They can be purchased online or at the party store.

There are lots of things you can give without spending lots of money:

- ❁ Put a personalized thank you note in a small frame which can be used later for a picture
- ❁ Small candles with a ribbon (to match the theme) tied around them are nice
- ❁ Fill a piece of tulle with potpourri and tie with a pretty ribbon
- ❁ A miniature plant in a miniature painted pot is adorable. Again match the colors to the theme

You'll have lots of ideas yourself and it will be lots of fun putting it together. Gather everyone around to help. Have FUN.

The Bachelor Party in the past has been a kind of "sow your wild oats" type party. But I think that has toned down a bit. It's all well and good to have a great time, but don't get carried away. Have the party well before the wedding. The groom doesn't want to be hung-over on the wedding day.

A Poker party would be fun with beer, wine, good snacks and cigars provided. Let anyone that needs to, spend the night. You might want to grill some burgers and hotdogs. A good time can be had by all and maybe the groom to be will win some money.

If your group is into golf it would be so much fun to go on a golf weekend. Find a nearby course with an inexpensive hotel close by. After the first eighteen holes, you'll be tired but I bet you'd go right back out there for another eighteen the next day.

You might all want to attend a sports event together to cheer for your favorite team. You'll think of more fun things that you would like to do.

The best man and the groomsmen should foot the bill for whatever the entertainment is going to be. So take it easy on the budget, but still have fun.

The Bachelorette Party can be so much fun. You could all go out and eat at a restaurant, but it would be a better time if you had a pajama party. Watching chick flicks, talking eating, or whatever you want to do would be a great time and it would be easier on the budget than going out. If you don't want to do that, go out to lunch with the girls. Whatever you do will be fun.

The Rehearsal Dinner traditionally was at a restaurant, but now a lot of the parents have it in their home. It is not nearly as costly as the restaurant. It should take place right after the rehearsal. The people attending should be the bride's attendants, the best man and groomsmen, both sets of parents, the bride and groom, of course and any out of town guests there are.

This is a good time to give your gifts to the bride's attendants, groomsmen and best man, ring bearer, flower girl, parents and each other.

Options to Save Big on Rings

Wedding rings symbolize the union of two people joined by the ring finger. Some people say the ring finger has an artery that leads straight to the heart. I don't know if that's true but it is romantic.

Once married most people don't take off their bands, as a sign of their faithfulness to each other. It's also a good idea to leave them on because they are surprisingly easy to lose.

Here is the buzz on saving a few bucks on your wedding bands:

❀ Simple gold bands are the cheapest. They start at around $50. They are also classic and elegant.

❀ Silver bands are modern and cheap.

- Don't buy the designer version of gold bands. That will save you a bunch.

- If you want white metal, opt for white gold. Platinum is almost double the price.

- You'll save almost half if you buy a coordinating set or trio (engagement ring, your wedding band and his band.)

- If you want a ring with a stone, don't forget semi-precious stones are beautiful. You don't have to have diamonds in your rings.

- Family wedding bands are a romantic heirloom and free.

- Shopping online can save you money. Make sure you pick a secure site with great customer service.

- Man made diamonds are perfect, considered the "real thing" and are a lot cheaper.

- Check out Swarovski Crystals. They are an inexpensive alternative to diamonds. Their rings are gorgeous and start at about $90. They really sparkle!

- Avoid a payment plan! You are better off to only look at rings you can afford to purchase.

- Buy a ring that is 14k gold rather than one that is 18k or 24k. 14k gold is cheaper and stronger.

- Shop at pawnshops or antique stores. The ring will be used but you can find some unique rings at a much lower price. You can also have it polished and resized.   .

- If you really want something more, make a plan, start saving now and decide to upgrade your wedding rings on your fifth anniversary or your tenth anniversary.

Diamond Wedding Rings:

Almost every bride wants a diamond wedding ring; after all it is very traditional. There are some things you should take into consideration before making the big purchase however.

Here are some of them:

- ❖ Know what you can afford and stick to your budget.

- ❖ Decide if you really need a ring with diamonds or if you would be as happy with a plain band and a diamond engagement ring. That would be less expensive.

- ❖ Make sure you deal with a reputable store or person when buying you rings.

- ❖ Make sure you get a certificate of authenticity from the dealer.

- ❖ Check out the guarantees.

- ❖ If you buy online check with the Internet Better Business Bureau and make sure the dealer can easily be contacted.

It is important to do lot of homework on diamonds. There are lots of things that you need to know about them…

- ❖ Clarity: This has to do with being flawless. The closer to flawless it is the more brilliant it is and the more expensive.

- ❖ Color: Until a stone crosses over to lots of color such as yellow, the more colorless it is the better and more expensive.

- ❖ Cut: The cut is how the diamond is faceted. Look at all the different cuts and find the one you love.

- ❖ Carat: Diamonds are measured in carat weight. The bigger ones of course are more expensive.

- ❖ Shape: Oval, Round, Square, Emerald, Princess, Marquis and Pear are some shapes to consider.

You can find lots of information online about diamond wedding rings and the precious metals they are set in. Gold and diamond rings are less expensive than a platinum diamond wedding ring. Don't forget that there is white gold, silver, 14k gold and 18k gold to choose from. Do some research and find yourself a beautiful diamond wedding ring set.

Antique Wedding Rings Are Stylish And Unique

Antique wedding rings offer a lot if you're looking for something different. They are unique and done with an artful hand. You will see a variety stones and other embellishments, which could include flowers, birds, hearts and other things. It's so romantic and the designs are beautiful.

Vintage rings come from different periods such as Art Nouveau, Art Deco, Victorian and Retro just to mention some. They are all beautiful in their own way.

You can find the rings at stores that sell estate jewelry and there are lots of stores online that deal in them. You may even find one for sale by an individual.

Do your homework and make sure you are dealing with a reputable store or individual and get a guarantee that it is authentic.

Look for a ring that you really love; you'll be wearing it for a long time.

If you have a ring handed down to you from family that is the best of all. It has a world of sentimental value and it is free and probably very beautiful. It doesn't get any better than that.

Beauty on the Cheap

You want every element of your wedding to be beautiful and that includes you. Looking great on your wedding day means you're relaxed, glowing and gorgeous. Becoming the bride you want to be depends on your skin, hair, makeup, and nails — and how you look in your dress. You will be immortalized in pictures taken that day so it's important to look and feel your best.

Take the time to work on yourself and start early. By the time your wedding day arrives, you will feel beautiful and be beautiful.

Don't worry, you don't have to spend a fortune to be stunning. We'll show you how to save big on beauty.

Diet

Changing your eating habits is a cheap and healthy way to look and feel great. Check out different diets online to see which is best suited for you. Don't forget to talk to your doctor before starting any diet or exercise program.

Here's some excellent diet advice to get you started.

Wedding Diet Tips:

> ➤ Decide on the amount of weight you need to lose. (1-2 pounds per week is a reasonable goal).
> ➤ Take before and after photos.
> ➤ Your goal is to lose fat…not muscle tissue so be sure to eat a good balance of protein, carbs and fats.
> ➤ Make getting in shape a priority and make time each day for your program.
> ➤ Pick a good start date and take a few days to prepare yourself.
> ➤ Track your progress and keep a food diary on Fitday.com. It's free and very helpful.
> ➤ Use a smaller plate for meals.
> ➤ Drink eight glasses of water a day.
> ➤ Add fruits and vegetables daily.
> ➤ Eat protein at every meal.
> ➤ Cut out all processed sugars.
> ➤ Order kids meals at a restaurant.
> ➤ Eat foods that are in season. They pack more nutrients.
> ➤ Don't use food to deal with stress. You could do your nails, go for a walk or call a friend.
> ➤ Chew your food at least 20 times.
> ➤ Slow down when you're eating.
> ➤ Nix fast food.
> ➤ Eat a good breakfast.

- Eat more soup. The non-creamy ones are filling and low-calorie.
- Use mustard instead of mayo.
- Cut out sodas, lemonade and sweet tea.
- Limit alcohol to weekends.
- Use an online support group.
- Read food labels carefully.
- Keep your eye on the prize. Imagine yourself walking down the aisle feeling healthy and fit.

Exercise

Exercise plays an important role in weight loss. If you don't exercise when you diet, you might lose lean tissue and end up looking flabby. Muscle makes you look good, fit and firm. On the flip side, if you work out every day of the week that doesn't mean you can eat whatever you want. It's important to strike a balance between diet and exercise. Again check with your doctor before starting any diet or exercise program.

Here are some tips to get you started.

Wedding Exercise Tips:

- Schedule your workouts every day. You'll be more likely to stick to it.
- Grab a partner to workout with you. It makes it easier and more fun.
- Set weekly goals.
- You don't have to join a gym to get results.
- Check out exercise videos at the library.
- Wear comfortable clothes and shoes.
- Sneak in exercise wherever you can by parking farther away at the store or super charging your housework.
- Don't drive when you can walk.
- Get up and move during TV commercials.

➤ Find something you like to do like playing tennis or swimming. Playing makes exercise fun.

➤ Consider weight training. It builds muscle and speeds up metabolism. You can even just use items around the house as your weights, for example soup cans.

➤ Check out Interval Training.

➤ Mix up your routine. It keeps you from getting bored and quitting and is good for your muscles.

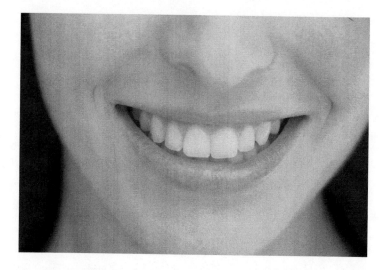

Teeth Whitening

You want your smile to be brilliant for your wedding and especially for your wedding pictures. There are tons of teeth whitening options available. You can even pick up a kit from the grocery store, which do work very well and are fairly inexpensive.

Here are the teeth whitening treatments available:

➤ In-office gel

➤ In-office laser bleaching

➤ At home custom fit trays

➤ Store-bought whitening strips

➤ In-mall whitening stands

> If you have Tetracycline stains, sensitive teeth or other issues, you may want to consult your dentist first. The dentist can provide a professional solution and monitor your progress.

Skincare

It's never too early to start your wedding skincare regimen. You can be your own skincare expert, look radiant and save a ton of money.

Once you set a date to be married, you should begin your skincare plan. Remember there will be lots of photos taken. You'll also be close to a lot of people, hugging and kissing.

Your first step is to establish a cleansing program that's right for your skin type. Cleanse in the morning and don't forget about make-up remover when you cleanse before bedtime. Regardless of your skin type...moisturize! The last step in your program should be exfoliating. This is so important for radiant skin.

Drinking water is crucial for your skin and your whole body for health. Make sure you are getting 8 to 10 glasses of water daily. Equally important for your skin is healthy fats. Include olive oil, or fish oil in your diet as well for luminous skin.

NOTE: Too much caffeine and not enough sleep can wreak havoc on your skin. So take extra good care of yourself before your big day.

Hair Removal

Hair removal therapies can be done by yourself or by a professional. If this is something you do yourself on a regular basis then by all means skip the salon and save the money. On the other hand, if you aren't skilled in hair removal or you want to try a new method, it's best to get professional help.

Here are some tips for getting smooth and hair-free for your wedding day.

The least expensive hair removal treatments are:

➤ Shaving
➤ Depilatories
➤ Home waxing
➤ Tweezing

If you are looking for methods that get longer lasting or more professional results you may want to consider these options:

➤ Salon waxing
➤ Threading
➤ Tweezing
➤ Electrolysis
➤ Laser Removal

TIP: You may want to try out your method of choice 6 to 8 weeks before the wedding to make sure you don't have any mishaps like rashes or bad reactions.

Manicures and Pedicures

The Hands:

You can make sure your fingers and toes look their best without spending a fortune. Now that you are wearing your engagement ring, you may have already begun taking extra special care of your fingernails. Don't forget your toes as well. Start your hand and foot care routine at least three months before your wedding.

There will be pictures of your hands on your big day and you may be wearing open-toed shoes. Plus you want to look fabulous down to every detail for your honeymoon.

You can achieve beautiful nails by working on them yourself. Most importantly keep them clean, neat and shaped properly. Keep them polished to protect them and prevent damage.

Keep hands exfoliated and moisturized.

Wear gloves when gardening or cleaning. Don't use your nails to help you perform tasks. Like the old saying goes..."Treat your nails like jewels NOT tools"

If you don't want to fuss with at home nail care, you may want to go to the salon for your Mani Pedi. Besides the traditional type of nail care you may want to try Shellac. Shellac is a soak-off hybrid between a gel and polish. You have to get it done at a salon specializing in Shellac manicures and pedicures. They are a little more expensive than a regular treatment but it lasts for up to three weeks and looks fresh and new until it is removed.

Acrylic nails are another option at the salon. Again more expensive than doing them yourself but they are stronger and last longer.

The Feet:

Your feet require just as much tender loving care...or maybe more. If you have any problems with your toenails you should see a doctor or other healthcare professional.

With feet, exfoliating and moisturizing are critical. Again you can do this yourself and save money or splurge and have pedicures done professionally. Either way have them done on a monthly basis for beautiful feet.

The Look:

A "French" is a classic wedding look. It is always in style and looks great on everyone. Some other classic looks include any soft colors like pink, beige, nude and clear pink. You may also opt for red, pink, wine or coral. If your style is a little more daring, don't be afraid to choose whatever color suits you.

NOTE: Make sure you have a few emergency nail items with you on the big day: a nail file, polish remover and polish...just in case.

If you take some extra time to pamper your hands and feet, you will be sure to look beautiful on your wedding day from head to toe.

Hair

Your hair is your crowning glory on your big day. Deciding on what style to wear is as important as choosing your dress. You may want to go natural or take this opportunity to do something extra special. Either way, here are some guidelines to follow to ensure you look your most gorgeous at your wedding.

Wedding Day Hair Advice:

- ❀ Plan early.
- ❀ Don't do anything too drastic or extreme.
- ❀ If experimenting with color, try a non-permanent one first.
- ❀ Deep condition your hair weekly.
- ❀ Consider a good hair supplement.
- ❀ Drink lots of water.
- ❀ Don't over wash you hair.
- ❀ Don't go overboard with hair spray the day of your wedding.

Choosing the right hairstyle for you:

Consider the formality and type of wedding you are having when choosing a hairstyle. Casual, loose looks are suitable for daytime or informal weddings, while up do's are more appropriate for a formal, evening look. Your hairstyle and headpiece should be complimentary to each other as well.

NOTE: Some hairstyles can add inches to your height. If you are on the shorter side, you could use this to your advantage.

Do A Test Run...Or Two

With wedding day hair, makeup and veil in place...have a friend take several photos of you at different angles. Make sure you like what you see. If anything isn't right, try something different and repeat the process until you are satisfied with your look.

> TIP: Don't just decide by looking in the mirror...take lots of pictures.

Also, remember to wear a button down shirt when you're getting your make-up and hair done on your big day.

Beautiful hair is a must for your wedding. With the right planning and some TLC, your hair will look gorgeous for your wedding. Be prepared for a ton of compliments.

Makeup

Wedding Day makeup is different than everyday makeup. If you are not proficient at getting glam...then seek professional help. If you can't afford a makeup artist for your big day, no worries, there are plenty of ways to get gorgeous and save money. Many department store makeup counters offer free make-up application. If you are partial to one brand this is great. If not, Sephora is a favorite place to get help. They offer free make-up application of numerous products and brands at all different prices.

Here are some wedding day make up must-haves:

- ❀ A foundation that stays put.
- ❀ Lip color with staying power.
- ❀ Mascara that doesn't run.
- ❀ Matte eye shadows.
- ❀ An eyelash curler.

- ❁ Powder to set make-up.
- ❁ Concealer.
- ❁ Highlighter for your brow bone.
- ❁ Perfect color blush.
- ❁ Eyebrow pencil.

Here are a few "DON'Ts" to keep in mind:

- ❁ Don't be too trendy.
- ❁ Don't wear shiny, frosted eye shadow.
- ❁ Don't forget your eyebrows.
- ❁ Don't wear too much makeup.
- ❁ Don't wear false eyelashes (unless you are VERY experienced with them).

Again, do a test run. Try products out well in advance. Get help if you need it. You want to look beautiful and feel confident.

Back Up Bag Essentials

The key to avoiding problems on your wedding day is to come prepared. Create a backup bag filled with essentials and emergency items. Give it to a bridesmaid or family member to hold for you or have someone stash in a place where you will have easy access to it on your big day.

Here are some items to you may want to have on hand:

Bottled water	Talcum powder
Breath Mints	Tissues
Eye drops	Blotting Papers
Hair spray	Mirrored compact
Hairpins	Nail file

Moist Wipes

Hand cream

Travel size sewing kit

Safety pins

Cotton swabs

Hem tape

Quick-drying glue (for broken shoe heels or fingernails)

Straws (so you can sip a drink without ruining your lipstick)

Fashion Tape (double sided tape for skin and fabric-great for holding bra straps in place or to keep a strapless gown from slipping)

White Chalk or cornstarch (to cover up any smudges on your gown)

Clear nail polish (for stocking runs)

An extra set of stockings

Throat lozenges

Aspirin

Band-Aids

Tampons

HINT: When purchasing your make-up, see if the sales person at the cosmetic counter will let you have samples of everything you're buying. They are the perfect size for your essentials bag!

Grooming the Groom

Modern day grooms understand how important wedding day grooming is for them. It's almost as important for them as it is for the bride...well almost.

Get the groom looking his best with these tips:

Consider a straight razor shave done at the barbershop.

Have the barber shave his neck to slightly below collar line.

Trim ear and nose hair.

Schedule a haircut about ten to fifteen days before the wedding date.

Clean and tidy nails are a must.

Groom eyebrows.

If doing a fake tan...practice well ahead of time.

If needed, wear an under-vest to absorb sweat.

Flower Power
on a Bargain Budget

When most people think of flowers, they think of romance. The romantic ambiance of your wedding depends on many factors – but flowers can definitely set the tone of style and formality.

Next to the wedding gown, flowers can also add the most visual impact to the wedding. The floral aspect of your wedding can also add an enormous impact on your budget – but they don't have to.

Flip through the pages of bridal magazines and you'll see that flowers for weddings range from huge arrangements to single stems. Either style can accomplish what you want for your wedding.

If you're having a destination wedding, the flowers may be included in the package. If you are having a theme wedding, your flowers should reflect the theme and season.

Everyone knows that roses suddenly become more expensive around Valentine's Day. This is also a normal occurrence when some florists discover that you're a bride-to-be. Suddenly, the same flowers you bought at the supermarket a week ago have increased in price at least 10%.

It's fun to shop for wedding flowers, but before you do, be sure that you've researched and visualized so that you know exactly what you want. Don't let a floral designer talk you into flowers that you just can't afford.

Read on to find ways to save when choosing flowers that will meet your vision – *and your budget.*

Adorning the Church or Ceremony Site

When you and your guests walk in to the site where your ceremony is to take place, you want the flowers to get "*wows*" from everyone.

Flowers chosen for the ceremony site should complement the color scheme of your wedding – from your wedding dress to the attendants' attire. Besides color, you'll want the flowers to harmonize with the season and the formality of the occasion.

The flowers of your vision that will adorn the place where your wedding vows are spoken might seem out of range after the prices give you a "wake up call."

There are ways to stretch the budget and get the flowers you really want for the ceremony site.

Budget Stretching Ideas:

❀ **What decorations might the ceremony site have on the day of your wedding?** - If you're being married in a church during the Christmas and Easter seasons, there may already be adornment such as fresh flowers and candles. Some churches have flowers every week that you may be able to use. You also may find someone else getting married at the church and split the cost of flowers with them.

❀ **Use an abundance of greenery in your decorations** - Ferns, leaves, twigs and evergreen branches will make the flowers in your arrangements look more plentiful and are available for a fraction of the cost.

❀ **Choose seasonal flowers** - If you don't know what will be in season on the day you've planned your wedding, ask your florist.

❀ **Use large, exotic flowers to make a visual impact** - Flowers such as the Stargazer Lily, hydrangea, large mums or sunflowers might cost more for a single stem, but by using them sparingly, you'll have a more impressive arrangement than a bunch of cheaper flowers - and actually come out ahead in cost.

❀ **Use long lengths of ribbon or tulle to decorate seating areas** - You can also purchase bow kits from a craft store and make beautiful bow decorations rather than decorating with flowers. If you really want to save money just decorate the first few pews or rows.

❀ **Potted plants are a great alternative to cut flowers** - Potted plants can add splashes of incredible color when grouped together, and they'll last long after the ceremony. It's a "green" way to decorate at your wedding and your home later.

❀ **Decorating Trellises and Arches is easy** - If you are having a garden wedding there may be an arch or a trellis involved. The easy way to decorate an arch or trellis is with artificial flowers attached to the arch or trellis with plastic cable ties purchased at your hardware store. You could also decorate with faux trailing greens like ivy or by using long strips of silky fabric or tulle to keep it simple and elegant.

* **Buy the flowers and decorate the site yourself** - Forgo the expensive florist designer and decorate the ceremony site yourself - or with the help of a friend. Lots of bargains can be found at wholesale prices if you're willing to do the footwork.

TIP: *When you have purchased your fresh flowers, cut off about an inch at an angle under water and put into a bucket of water until you're ready to arrange them.*

You can also be a prudent bride by having someone cart the flowers at the ceremony to the reception site. This can get a little tricky though, so be sure you have enough time and someone you trust to do the deed.

Bridal Bouquets On a Budget

Huge bridal bouquets are lovely but can be expensive. Single-stem flowers are elegant and cheap. Another good money saving idea is a hand-tied bouquet because it is gorgeous and easy to do it yourself. One glance in bridal and celebrity magazines will tell you that brides are opting to make a statement rather than investing in elaborate bouquets.

Just as a gigantic handbag looks comical when carried by a very short woman, a too-large bridal bouquet seems out of place when carried by a smaller bride. So be sure that your bridal bouquet matches your stature.

Cost saving tips when choosing your bouquet:

* **Choose miniature flowers** – most can be purchased for a fraction of the cost of larger flowers.

* **Add a couple of large, exotic flowers for effect** – A large zinnia bloom or spider-mum can be a striking addition to your bridal bouquet.

- **A single gorgeous bloom is elegant and easy** - a Calla Lilly (cut out stamens to avoid stains), sunflower, hydrangea, rose, peony, or bird of paradise would all be beautiful with just a nice ribbon around it. How simple is that?

- **Herbs can be the answer to expensive flowers** – Herbs are both fragrant and stunning and can make for a very inexpensive bouquet. Herbs also symbolize emotions and various aspects of life.

- **Skip the bouquet toss** – Keep your bouquet as a keepsake of the day or order a smaller, less expensive bouquet to toss, if that's a tradition you'd like to keep.

- **Use silk flowers – or mix them with fresh** – Silk flowers can be almost indistinguishable from fresh and you can purchase them at a local craft store or from Internet web sites in bulk. If you must have fresh flowers, consider mixing them with silk ones.

- **Check supermarkets and warehouse clubs for deals** -Don't forget supermarkets when it comes to choosing a bridal bouquet. Many have expert flower departments that can put together the bouquet of your dreams for very little cost.

- **Consider online florists** – Check out online floral sites. Some have excellent deals. Just make sure you check their policies before ordering.

TIP: *The bridal bouquet of fresh flowers should be made just a few hours before the wedding, sprayed with a little water and put into the refrigerator. Be sure and have it to her in time for the pictures.*

Finally, when shopping for wedding bouquet flowers, choose wisely. If you're using a florist, be sure that he or she understands that you're on a tight budget, but that you want to do everything you can to get what you want and still stick to the numbers.

Other Flora and Fauna Considerations

Smart budgeting doesn't mean that you have to compromise on ensuring that your wedding day is filled with beautiful sights and smells that flowers provide. Depending on your taste and how much effort you're willing to put forth, you can create a magical setting for your wedding for very little money.

Besides the bridal bouquet and decorations for the wedding ceremony site, here are some other floral considerations:

❀ Bridesmaids' bouquets.

❀ Mothers' corsages.

❀ Boutonnieres.

❀ Centerpieces for reception tables.

❀ Garlands, Pomanders and Topiaries.

These considerations alone could tax your budget for well over $2,000.

Here's how you can keep the budget intact for $300.00 or less and still create a stunning visual impact:

Bridesmaids Bouquets:

❀ Visit floral shops a year before your wedding - You may be able to find an array of inexpensive flowers you've never heard of or seen before that will be available during the season of your wedding.

❀ Gather your bridesmaids to make the bridal bouquets - Purchase the flowers of your choice and make the bouquets yourself. Keep it simple and use lots of greenery and ribbons to tie it all together.

❀ Bridesmaids' bouquets should be complimentary- The bridesmaids carry smaller, coordinating bouquets, which makes them cheaper. For instance, if the bride has roses in her bouquet, the bridesmaids can have just one rose with other less expensive flowers in their bouquets.

Mothers' Corsages:

✿ Purchase small, simple corsages for the mothers - Look at supermarket flower departments to see what you can find for the least amount of money.

✿ Make them yourself- Get one nice large bloom such as an orchid and follow the "To Do" Boutonniere instructions.

Boutonnieres:

✿ Be creative with the boutonnieres - Small sprigs of fragrant herbs or other inexpensive, but attractive flowers make interesting and unique boutonnieres for the guys. You can use almost anything to make a boutonniere and you can do it yourself. Think about shells, acorns, leaves or anything you can imagine. If you are going to use a flower...it's nice to match it with the bride's bouquet.

How to Make a Boutonniere:

Just cut the flower stem to about three inches

Wrap with floral tape and that's it.

Include a pearl head pin with it.

Centerpieces:

✿ Use pretty glass bowls- Fill half full of water and float a single blossom on top.

✿ Giant vases filled with branches of colorful leaves or berries — If you're having a fall or winter wedding, this can be an especially attractive way to celebrate the season of your wedding.

- ❀ **Use potted plants for centerpieces** – You can purchase potted plants for much less than cut flowers, and keep them to decorate your home after the wedding.

- ❀ **Use your warehouse clubs** – They offer flowers at a discounted rate all year long.

- ❀ **Large bouquets** – Make bouquets with big bunches of Baby's Breath only. It looks high end if it is large and makes a beautiful statement. For the head table you can do the same thing but add a few roses.

- ❀ **From your garden**- Flowers from your own garden (or a friend's) are free. If you are lucky enough to have access, by all means take advantage of your good fortune.

- ❀ **Flowering branches**- Bougainville, dogwood or azaleas make stunning centerpieces. You don't need a lot of them to make a big impact.

- ❀ **One bloom**- Lots of small, pretty containers with one bloom can be used for lovely wedding centerpieces.

- ❀ **No Water**- Hibiscus blooms can be put around on a table without any water. They must be picked and used one the same day. They will last for one day only.

- ❀ **Petals Only**- Rose petals can be spread on the table. You can scatter them freely or shape them in a heart, circle, monogram or whatever pattern you choose. Get roses that have seen better days and are on sale. Silk rose petals can be pretty inexpensive as well.

- ❀ **Silk Flowers**- Silk flowers are not always cheaper but sometimes you can find them on sale. Choosing a cluster of flowers as opposed to a single bloom stretches your dollar even further. Another advantage of silk flowers is that you can make your centerpieces well in advance.

- ❀ **Non-Floral**- For lots of great non-floral centerpiece ideas see Chapter 13.

TIP: Again, when you have purchased your fresh flowers, cut off about an inch at an angle under water and put into a bucket of water until you're ready to arrange them.

Garlands, Pomanders and Topiaries:

Garlands- You can purchase silk flower garlands to decorate the reception hall, the chair backs or run them down the length of your table. Check online for pre-made garlands. There are lots of inexpensive choices.

Pomanders- Pomanders or kissing balls make a beautiful statement. You can make them yourself with fresh flowers and a floral oasis or with silk flowers and Styrofoam. Check our website at www.cheap-chic-weddings.com for instructions on making a silk pomander. They make gorgeous centerpieces, chair ornaments or hanging decorations.

Topiaries- Topiaries are perfect for an entrance or to frame the Head Table. Small ones are ideal for centerpieces. You can buy them, rent them or make them.

These are just a few good ideas that can save money on your wedding flowers. Wander through craft stores and florist shops to gather even more dollar-saving ideas that might work for your wedding style.

You're bound to find ways you never thought possible to pare down the floral piece of the "budget pie" if you give yourself enough time and are really committed to the effort of saving wedding dollars.

Favorite Favors for Less

Wedding favors say thank you to your guest and I'm glad you're here (without spending a fortune). Choosing favors is fun and easy when you consider the style of your wedding. There is also the question...to have or have not. If your budget is really tight, you may forgo the favors altogether. No one will even notice because everyone will be having so much fun. Can you really do without favors? The answer is YES...if you want to. You could shave off a hundred bucks or more by not having them. If you do decide to give out favors, you definitely won't break the bank with cheap wedding favors.

Here are wedding favor ideas that can be done inexpensively:

- 🌸 Small flower arrangements at each place setting could double as wedding favors and table decorations. I have bought glass containers at thrift stores for twenty-five cents. They don't have to match. If you're using artificial flowers you could use terracotta pots.

- 🌸 Divinity fudge makes delicious cheap wedding favors. Wrapped up in white tulle and tied with a white ribbon it would be beautiful. Add a tag; you make yourself, with a little message like "Love is divine". Cut out the tag with scallop scissors and punch a hole for the ribbon. One warning, divinity doesn't come out well in high humidity.

- 🌸 Candles made in seashells are pretty for a beach wedding or any wedding for that matter. Melt some beeswax but don't get it too hot. Pour it into the shell and add a wick. Get directions at your craft store. If you live near the sea gather shells yourself. Shells can also be purchased by the bag.

- 🌸 Regular candles are nice too for cheap wedding favors. Wrap in tulle and tie with ribbon. Stick a small flower in the ribbon.

- 🌸 Tree seedlings, such as citrus or any kind of tree, are something everybody would love. They will always remember your wedding with this unique wedding favor idea. Wrap the plastic pot to disguise.

- 🌸 Small frames for later use can also serve as place cards or to hold a message from you.

- 🌸 Flower seedlings or seed packets are nice wedding favors. Wrap in any way that is appropriate for your wedding. Tie with ribbon, raffia or paper ribbon.

- 🌸 Make wine glass markers from wire and beads. You can find instructions at the craft store. One is enough for a wedding party favor. Place in a small box and tie with ribbon.

- 🌸 Sachets made from lavender. Make a small bag from lace. Sew up three sides, put the lavender in and sew up fourth side. Attach a small silk flower. Potpourris in drawstring bags made of lace or tulle are pretty. They smell nice too. You can use any kind of bag that's easy for you to make.

❀ Everybody loves herbs. Buy small ones and place plastic container right into a small terracotta pot. Put some moss around the top to disguise the plastic planter. Include a pretty tag with instructions for care and attach to a ribbon tied around the pot.

❀ A strawberry plant is another live wedding favor idea. It can be presented in the same way as an herb. Anything of this nature that is in season is appreciated.

❀ Candies, such as M&Ms in your wedding colors, Kisses or Hugs, mints, a wonderful piece of chocolate or any kind that you would like, look great in a cupcake liner. They come in different sizes and colors.

❀ Bookmarks are becoming very popular for wedding favors that your guests will appreciate and keep for a long time.

❀ Make coasters using tiles from a home store. Mod Podge scrap booking paper to the tiles. Tie a ribbon around coasters.

❀ Mason Jars filled with store bought jam, honey or peanuts is a great favor and inexpensive. You can embellish jars with ribbon or raffia.

Chocolate is a good choice for most as most people like to eat it and it's easy to pull off an elegant look on a budget. The only time you may want to stay away from chocolate is at a beach wedding (if it's warm) or any other outdoor wedding where the climate may get hot. You can go a few ways here with chocolate favors.

You can make your own chocolates or purchase packaged chocolates and wrap them in a creative way. If you decide to tackle making them on your own, it is easier than ever. Craft stores, warehouse stores and the Internet carry several choices of molds, bags, chocolate melts and containers. The world is your oyster on this.

Here are some suggestions on making your chocolate wedding favors special:

- ❀ Make your own heart shaped chocolate lollipops.

- ❀ Dip knotted or rod pretzels in white or dark chocolate. You can add a cute note to knotted pretzels about "tying the knot". While the chocolate is warm, you can add any toppings you like. Crushed nuts, sprinkles, nonpareils, and crushed cereal all work well.

- ❀ For a country theme: place chocolate candies a small cute flowerpot.

- ❀ For the tropical look: place candies in flat seashells.

- ❀ Cut out homemade chocolate brownies with cookie cutters and wrap in cellophane or wrap like a present. Who doesn't love brownies? This is our favorite edible wedding favor.

- ❀ Dip shortbread cookies in melted chocolate, let cool and wrap. This works great with sandwich cookies too! You can "glue" on smaller candies for decoration with more melted chocolate.

Fall is a beautiful time of year for a wedding and really lends itself to great fall wedding favors. Have a little get-together to make your own fall wedding favors. Your family and friends would be happy to help and they may come up with some dynamite ideas.

There are of course lots of gorgeous natural items you could use to create your wedding favors.

They include:

- ❀ Autumn leaves
- ❀ Sunflowers
- ❀ Pumpkins
- ❀ Twigs
- ❀ Dried Beans
- ❀ Berries
- ❀ Indian corn
- ❀ Raffia
- ❀ Gourds
- ❀ Nuts
- ❀ Fruit

Some man-made items include:

- Spray paint (i.e. gold)
- Fabric paint pen (Fabric paint in a plastic bottle with a tip. Find it at the craft store)
- Artificial fruit and flowers
- Glass containers
- Tulle
- Metallic pens
- Terracotta pots
- Stamps for putting on a design
- Ribbon

Some fall favors you can make:

- A cornucopia made with a waffle ice cream cone, candy and nuts. Simply fill the cone with any type candy and/or nuts. Tie on a ribbon that coordinates with your color scheme.

- A candleholder made from a mini pumpkin. Just hollow out a hole large enough to put a small candle in (a color to match your color scheme). The candle should fit snugly. Decorate around the hole in an anyway you like. Maybe with a paint pen or metallic pen. But, don't use anything that would be a fire hazard.

- Small terracotta pots filled with candy corn. Paint the pot any color you'd like and decorate in anyway you want. Put a plastic liner inside. Use plastic wrap you get at the supermarket. The pot can also double as a place card. Just write the name of the guest on each one. Use a metallic pen or paint pen.

- Use a small terracotta pot for a pretty leaf arrangement. Use floral foam or Styrofoam cut to fit the pot. Put in beautiful colored leaves and you could incorporate some acorns sprayed painted gold. Acorns or dried beans could cover the Styrofoam to keep it from showing through.

- Use tulle in pretty fall colors as a wonderful holder for candy or nuts. Make an 8 in. circle and place the candy or nuts in the middle. Gather up the tulle and tie with a pretty ribbon.

- Pots decorated with leaf stamps can be a holder for seed packets.

Candle wedding favors make great gifts. When you give away a candle, you know that most everyone will use it.

Candle wedding favors are really a great bargain and there are a lot of options when choosing candles as favors. You can go one of two ways here. You can make your own candle favors or purchase them.

If you make your own, you may end up spending as much or more that purchasing finished favors.

Many resources on the Internet offer beautiful candle favors at very reasonable prices. We have seen some as low as $1- $2. The prices on almost all of the places we found went down even more when you order large quantities.

The up side of making your own is that you can always do it exactly as you want to. You can use containers that you choose and colors that you choose.

You can do something as simple as a votive candle in a glass votive holder, wrapped in an organza bag and tied with coordinating ribbon.

You can also do elaborate hand beading, decorating, and wrapping. It just depends on your budget and your available time and talent.

If you choose to order candle wedding favors, there are a many to choose from.

Here are some that you will find...

- ✿ Mini wedding cake candles
- ✿ Mini Pear Candles
- ✿ Varieties of wrapped votives in many styles and colors
- ✿ Monogrammed candles
- ✿ Candles in jars

If there is a special theme to your wedding, use anything that would carry out that theme. For example, you could use delicate teacups wedding favors for a Victorian inspired reception. We hope we've given you some ideas for cheap wedding favors you can use or that will inspire you to come up with your own.

Tip on Ordering Your Favors:

If you are ordering favors online, make sure you will receive them in plenty of time before the wedding just in case there are any mishaps.

Extra Tips:

➤ Dual-purpose favors really stretch your dollar. For example, you can burn candles as table decorations and then let your guests take one home as a favor. Or you can place a small vase with a single flower in it as decoration and then give them out at the end of the night.

➤ Edible favors are easy and cheap and definitely won't be left behind.

➤ Don't forget...if you are really on a tight budget, SKIP the wedding favors and don't look back. It's okay.

Saving Money while Saving Memories...Tricks for Pics and Video

One aspect of weddings never really changes, and that is that every couple has the desire to preserve memories of their wedding day with photos and videos. Your wedding photos create memories for a lifetime. Hiring a professional is your top choice here and there are plenty of options to avoid over spending on your photography and videography. Hiring a professional ensures that you are getting someone who has the proper equipment, the experience and is a skilled person with an artistic eye.

Be prepared by knowing what you want. Know the lingo...do you want formal style photos, photojournalistic style or a mix of both? Is the person you are interviewing the person coming to shoot your wedding? How much time will they spend with you? Does he or she use film or digital?

As with all of your other planning, have a PLAN! Discuss with your future spouse how much you want to spend on photography, how you want your photos to look, and how you are going find the right photographer for you.

We recommend you interview as many photographers as time allows. Get recommendations and referrals from friends and family members, and do your homework before you get out there. Be sure to ask to see the photographer's work.

Saving Money When Hiring a Pro Photographer

There are different places to find a photographer. Some work out of a studio and some are freelance. There are some photographers who work as a photographer as a second job. It's a good idea to look at your choices as some have more overhead and other expenses than others.

While you want to save as much money as you can, cheapest is not always the best way to go. Try to find the best photographer for you and your budget!

Money saving tips:

- ❀ Remember to be strong and stick to your plan. Never feel like you HAVE to purchase anything you don't want or cannot afford.

- ❀ Be upfront about your budget and ask him or her to work with you so that everyone wins!

- ❀ Don't be afraid to negotiate. The photographer may be able to throw in extra shots, prints or time.

- ❀ This is another area where getting married any other day than Saturday may play in your favor. Ask your photographer for a discount if your wedding is on an off day.

- ❀ Have a professional shoot for less time. Have him or her shoot only your ceremony for instance.

- ❀ Photographers own the rights to your photos, but many are willing to sell you the proofs or digital disc along with the rights to print photos yourself.

- Wedding photographers offer package deals. Usually there is a basic package and then prices go up as packages get bigger and more elaborate. This is where you can cut some of the expense by leaving out extras.

- Many packages include an album made by the photographer. You can opt to get prints and put the album together yourself.

- Even better, ask a scrapbooker friend to put one together as a gift to you!

- Do you have a product or service that you can barter? Ask the photographer if he is willing to consider bartering his service.

- Some photographers come with an assistant or second photographer. If it can save you money, cut the extra person.

- Ask a university student to shoot your wedding. Be sure to see his samples of work!

- Check out sites like Craigslist.org and Guru.com.

- Many cities have photography schools and photography clubs. These can be excellent resources.

The Contract

Understanding the contract between you and your photographer is very important. The contract ensures that everyone is getting what is expected and that everything is covered. It is there to protect you and the photographer. If at any point you do not understand or are uncomfortable with the contract, speak up or go to someone else.

Wedding photography contracts can vary at different photographers, but they cover basically the same things.

A wedding photography contract can include the following...

- All the basic info about you and your fiancé.
- Location details like place names, addresses and times.
- Description of what the photographer will be doing.
- Package details.
- Type of photography that will be used.

- ❀ Money details like deposit and payment info.
- ❀ Any additional fees that may come up.
- ❀ What do all of the fees include?
- ❀ Backup and contingency plans. Backup equipment and photographers should be available.
- ❀ Refund and Cancellation policies.
- ❀ Rights regarding the images. What are you getting? Digital files, negatives, prints only?
- ❀ Model Release of images. Photographers may ask to use your images for advertising, websites or other marketing.
- ❀ Any restrictions
- ❀ Any wish list items from you
- ❀ Arbitration plan. Who will settle any disputes?
- ❀ Delivery time of the final product.

Understanding your contract may save you money in the long run. Know what you are getting and when you are getting it. Don't be surprised later. Be sure you communicate clearly with your photographer and let them know immediately if any thing changes!

Pacing of Photographs

If you have hired a professional photographer or are planning to, your photographer will very likely have his/her own way that they like to pace the photo taking. A professional will know how to make things flow properly when it comes to weddings.

Talk with your photographer about how your wedding day is planned out and discuss the potential shot list (see shot list). Depending on how the photographer is charging you, whether by package or time, you will all be able to determine a good pace. It's a good idea to convey what you want because time only allows so many photos to be taken.

Generally, photos are taken as the bride and/or groom prepare for the wedding, at the ceremony, between the ceremony and reception and at the reception. The photos taken between the ceremony and reception are traditionally posed, while the rest of the day's photos are more candid.

If you are not hiring a professional, it's best to follow a plan that a photographer would. Be prepared with your pacing and how much time to allow, and always have a shot list.

Shot List

Planning out your shots will certainly help the day of photo taking go smoothly. If you are hiring a professional photographer, he or she will have a shot list prepared. Be sure to communicate any shot ideas that you like that may not be on the list.

Here are some shot list ideas:

Before the wedding...

➤ The dress hanging on a pretty hanger or draped over a chair.

➤ Bride leaving home.

➤ Bride getting dressed.

➤ Zipping, lacing or buttoning up the dress.

➤ Maid of Honor or Mom fastening bride's necklace or adjusting dress.

➤ Maid of Honor or Mom putting on the veil.

➤ Bride's Veil

➤ Bride's Garter.

➤ Bride's clean shoes.

➤ Bride and maids doing their makeup and hair.

➤ Bride gazing out of a window.

➤ Bride with parents and/or siblings.

➤ Bride with bridesmaids.

➤ Bride and Parents in limo/going to ceremony.

- Groom tying his tie.
- Groom with Parents.
- Groom with siblings.
- Groom with groomsmen.
- Groom with Best Man.
- Groom checking his watch.
- Boutonnieres and corsages being put on.

At the Ceremony:

- Exterior of ceremony site.
- Guests arriving.
- Mother of the bride being escorted in.
- Mother of the groom being escorted in.
- Grandmothers being escorted in.
- Each Bridesmaid and maid of honor walking down the aisle with groomsmen and best man.
- Flower girl and Ring Bearer walking down the aisle.
- Groom waiting for the bride at the altar.
- Wedding party waiting at the altar.
- Bride and Father as they start to enter.
- Groom seeing the bride for the first time.
- Father and bride walking down the aisle.
- Father giving away bride.
- The Officiant.
- The altar or the front.
- Any ceremony singers or musicians.
- Vows exchange.
- Rings exchange.
- Hands and Rings close-up.
- The kiss.

- Bride and groom being introduced as husband and wife.
- Bride and groom coming down the aisle.
- Guests throwing birdseed/blowing bubbles/throwing flower petals.
- Receiving Line.
- Bride and groom in front of ceremony site.
- Bride and groom leaving.
- Bride and groom in back seat.

Between the ceremony and reception (traditionally posed shots):

- Bride alone-full length and close-up.
- Bride and groom together-full length and close-up.
- Bride with Maid of Honor.
- Bride with bridesmaids.
- Bride and groom with her parents.
- Bride and groom with his parents.
- Bride and groom with any combination of family members.
- Bride and groom with bridesmaids.
- Bride and groom with groomsmen.
- Bride and groom with full wedding party.
- Bride and groom with flower girl and ring bearer.
- Bride with groomsmen.
- Groom with bridesmaids.

At the reception:

- Outside of the reception site.
- Bride and groom arriving at the reception.
- Close-ups of details like seating cards, centerpieces, guest book, favors, etc.
- Bride and groom being introduced.
- Head Table.

- Parent's and siblings tables.
- Guest tables.
- Gift table.
- Decorations
- Musicians and/or DJ.
- The wedding cake.
- The groom's cake.
- Bride and groom visiting each table.
- All toasts and speeches.
- Bride and groom toasting and sipping champagne.
- Bride and groom's first dance.
- Bride/dad and Groom/mom dances.
- Parents dancing.
- All other special dances.
- Buffet or a plated dinner.
- Bride and groom cutting the cake.
- Bride and groom "serving" each other cake.
- The bouquet toss.
- Groom retrieving the garter from bride.
- The garter toss.
- Garter being put on bouquet receiver.
- All guests in a group photo.
- The getaway car.
- Bride and groom waving from car.
- Rear of car leaving.

This shot list is just a sample of the different great wedding shots you might want. Be sure to tell your photographer of any other shots you would like. You will likely save money if you keep your shot list to only those you really want.

Do it Yourself Photography

Of course you won't be doing it yourself...this means that you will be using someone other than a professional photographer. If your budget just does not allow for a professional to come in OR you will be using a professional for part of the day, then this is for you.

Are you planning on having a friend or family member shoot your pictures? Here are a few tips:

- ❀ Make sure you have an extra camera ready or better yet an extra photographer.
- ❀ Have extra memory cards ready.
- ❀ Be sure your batteries are charged and have an extra if you can.
- ❀ Have a tripod handy.
- ❀ Go over your desired shot list with the person taking photos.
- ❀ If possible, scout the area together ahead of time.
- ❀ Give them an idea of how and where to do candid shots.
- ❀ If you have only one photographer, assign someone to be a helper.
- ❀ Have your DIY photographer study other wedding photos before the actual wedding day.

These are tried and true tips! If a professional is shooting your ceremony and/or formal portraits, you still need to consult with your main DIY photographer.

These days, plenty of people have great digital cameras. Ask as many people as possible to shoot photos for you. The more shots taken, the better.

Consider looking for potential photographers just outside of your friends and family group and look for local photography clubs and classes and find a budding pro for no or little cost.

One last tip...when asking others to take photos for you, have a place for folks to upload their digital photos to share with you. This can be done on your personal wedding website or through a file sharing site on the Internet. Of course, they can also give you copies on discs.

Composition

If you hire a professional, you will not have to worry about the composition of your photos. If you are doing it yourself, you can use these hints:

- ❀ Use the rule of thirds. The rule of thirds is where you imagine that your photo is divided into nine squares (like a tic-tac-toe board over it). You place your subject on one of the lines or at the intersection of those lines. Some cameras have a rule of thirds overlay setting.
- ❀ Or get creative and break the rule!
- ❀ Pay attention to your backgrounds! You don't want a tree to appear to be growing from the bride's head!
- ❀ Frame your photos carefully and with some thought.
- ❀ When taking group photos, have a helper get them together.
- ❀ Elevate yourself for some photos.
- ❀ Get close up for nice shots of one or two or three people. Fill the frame with them.

Photo Booth Fun

Having a photo booth at your wedding reception can be loads of fun! There are a few choices if you'd like to have one. First, there are professional companies that rent booths out for weddings and other occasions.

You can also go the route of making your own photo booth. The best place to find good instructions on building a booth is on the Internet. This project could take special skills and most likely some help.

A simpler do it yourself plan for a photo booth could involve just hanging a pretty cloth or paper backdrop and setting up a camera and lights. You can use a remote for your camera or have one or two volunteers shoot the photos.

Black and White Photos

Many Brides and Grooms love to have some shots from their wedding in Black and White! Black and white photos have a classic; elegant look and can look modern at the same time. Black and white photos can produce a clean look and really bring out detail that you would not notice in color photos. Black and white photos also make wedding photos seem timeless and definitely romantic.

There are a few different ways to get some of your photos in black and white. First, ask your professional photographer to include some black and white shots for your package. Second, for those of you who will not be using a pro, ask the person shooting for you if their digital camera can shoot in a black and white mode. You also have the option with digital to change a color photo to black and white after the wedding day. There are computer programs that can help with this transformation.

If you have friends or family shooting with film, you can still buy black and white film and have it processed.

Decisions, Decisions

Deciding what to keep and print and what not to print is really tough. In the interest of saving money, it's probably best to make your decisions based on your budget and restrain from picking tons of extra photos after you have already decided on a package back when you hired your photographer. The beauty of digital files and negatives is that more photos can always be printed later.

Who gets what?

It is likely that some of your friends and family members will want photos from your wedding. This is a time that you will have to be strong and stick to your budget. Nicely offer opportunities for your guests to buy photos or make copies for themselves.

If you have budgeted for gifts, consider giving your parents or other folks involved in the wedding a framed photo or small photo album.

Photo Sharing

This is why we love the Internet...consider sharing your digital files on the Internet so everyone interested can see the photos and/or make copies. You can share your photos on your personal wedding website, social network sites like Facebook or photo sites like Shutterfly.com. Sharing photos online can be free or very low cost.

Communicate a place where your guests can share their photos with YOU. Place cards on the reception tables instructing them where to upload their photos. You can also post this info on your personal wedding website.

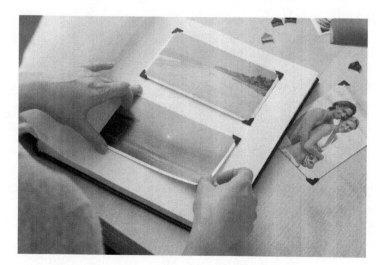

Keeping the Memories

If you have opted to hire a professional photographer, he or she is very likely to offer you some kind of wedding album with your package price. This is a wonderful option for those who either have the money to do it or are not very comfortable with putting the photos in an album.

There are alternatives to getting your album done professionally. You can print the photos yourself and place them in a chosen album. You may have a friend who does scrap booking. If so, ask them to help you put together a wedding album. This option can be especially special and may give that person a chance to do this as a gift to you. Craft stores and discount stores have great supplies available.

The scrapbook style album also allows you to add things that you cannot place in an ordinary album. Use magazine and newspaper clippings, printed vows, your invitation, pressed flower petals, napkins and honeymoon brochures to add that personal touch!

Even non-techie types have great success putting together digital online albums and photo books. There are many sites on the Internet that offer this service. Usually membership is free and you can upload your photos and use their templates to get on your way.

The best thing about these sites is that you can create an album or book exactly to your liking! You can mix and match looks, edit your photos, crop photos and use graphics and captions. Online photo sites offer a wide range of price points and truly have something for everyone.

Popular sites, like Shutterfly.com, can also be a great one-stop shop. They offer all kinds of cards, announcements, gift ideas and even free personal wedding websites!

Lights! Camera! Action! Videography!

Even more than photos, a good video of the action on your wedding day is a precious record that you'll enjoy over and over. It's a way to capture the looks; movements and sounds of loved ones on that special day of your life.

A video that includes moments of you laughing with a grandmother or special aunt or dancing with your father will be priceless to you in the years to come.

We believe that any video is better than no video at all. So budget for the best videographer possible.

If your budget allows and you are hiring a professional to shoot video, consider these tips:

- Get recommendations from friends, family members and even your photographer
- Don't be afraid to shop around for the videographer that's right for you.
- Ask lots of questions. How many cameras does he use, what kind of lighting, his editing process, who will own the rights to the video, what will the final DVD look like?
- Ask to see his or her work
- Read and review the contract carefully!
- Don't be afraid to express what your expectations are.

If you desire video footage of your wedding and simply do not have a budget for it, think about some do-it-yourself options. Have a friend or family member take over the video job. Like we said, some is better than none!

Mix it up. Hire a pro for a portion of the day. Have them attend the ceremony, and then ask for a friend to do the reception, or vice versa. Another money saving tip is to ask the videographer to use only one camera. Cutting out the assistant and additional camera can save big bucks.

You can also save money by hiring a university film student or a videographer that works from home and is not necessarily connected to an expensive studio.

Weather you choose a professional videographer or an official helper(s); convey to them what you want your video to include. Don't forget guest interviews, family traditions, important dances, toasts, etc. Give your videographer a list of your wishes and include the itinerary of the day.

There are plenty of software programs that allow you to try your hand at editing your video yourself. If you saved by not getting a professional, then perhaps have an editing service do it for you.

Registries and Gifts Including Tactful Ways to Receive Cash

In 1924 Marshall Fields started a wedding registry so that brides-to-be could register for their china, crystal and silver pattern. Most people today live a more casual lifestyle but it is good that there is something for everyone.

Fifty years ago Chuck Williams, who founded Williams Sonoma, started making a list for the couples that were to be married. They picked out things they liked and wanted and when the future wedding guest came in he helped them with exactly what the couple needed

These things brought us to where we are now. There are many registries today with everything you could possibly imagine. You can pretty much be assured that you will get what you want. The wedding guests will also be happy that they know exactly what to give you and that it will be appreciated

Be sure you pick a registry that has the things that you really can't live without. A lot of the registries have a big variety; it's a good idea to choose more than one registry but probably no more than two or three. It is much easier when your guest don't have to look in too many registries. They will like that. Keep in mind when you're picking gifts not everyone can afford an expensive gift. Choose different prices for your guests to select from. They do want to give you something that will make you happy.

When should you register? Six months ahead would be good. That gives the guests plenty of time and it would be especially convenient if they wanted to buy a shower gift also.

There are lots of stores that have wedding registries. Here is a sample of stores with registries:

- ❀ Crate and Barrel
- ❀ Williams Sonoma
- ❀ Tiffany & Co.
- ❀ Walmart.com
- ❀ MyRegistry.com (includes lots of stores)
- ❀ Macy's
- ❀ Belk.com

- ❀ Pottery Barn
- ❀ JC Penney
- ❀ Bed Bath and Beyond
- ❀ Sears
- ❀ Target
- ❀ Bloomingdales

There are many online registries. Do some research of your favorite places to see if they have bridal registries online. Surfing the web makes it super easy for your guests to pick your gift.

There are some unusual registries that you might want to check out. Listed below are some of them:

Honeymoon Registries

Mortgage Wedding Registries (these are practical and very helpful if you want to save for a down payment on a home...i.e. Sun Trust Bank}

Home Improvement Registries (like Home Depot and Lowe's)

Some Charities offer registries

Tactful Ways To Ask For Cash Gifts

Maybe you and your fiancée have been living together and have your household all set up. Maybe you want to save up for a down payment on a home. Whatever the reason, there is really no stigma attached to cash gifts.

How do you let your guests know that you're not going to be registered anywhere and would like cash instead of gifts? The best way is by word-of-mouth. Let guests ask your family or attendants what you need or want. If you are not registered, they can spread the word about your preference.

Another alternative is cash gift registries. You can register for all kinds of things like vacations or music lessons etc. Your guests can make cash gifts towards the items on the registry.

NOTE: Any mention of a wedding gift or registry on your invitations is a BIG no-no!

Gifts for Others

"Others" are all the people in the wedding party including the bride and groom. There are also both sets of parents, the bride's attendants, the groomsmen, the flower girl and ring bearer.

All of these people have been great support for you throughout the whole process of getting ready for your big day. Of course you want to show your appreciation to all of them with a gift

They are all good friends of yours so you probably know what they all like. Focus on any hobbies they have and how they love to spend their time. Something meaningful to your friendship with them would be nice.

Some Suggestions:

For Each Other jewelry is always a good bet. A bottle of really good champagne for the honeymoon is special. Luggage is very practical.

For the Parents think about this, a gift certificate for a night out at a nice restaurant. Theatre tickets or a book of movie tickets are fun. Make sure it's something you know they would really enjoy

For the Bride's Attendants here are some things that girls love. A gift certificate for a   manicure or pedicure is always appreciated. Cosmetic bags are useful. What would really be great is a charm that is a keepsake of your wedding and friendship.

For the Groomsmen think about their lifestyle, what their favorite sport is and any special pastime they have. There are shirts and t-shirts with the name of their favorite team, money clips and key chains. Don't forget the good old gift certificate.

For the Flower Girl and Ring Bearer make sure their gifts are age appropriate. You can find so many inexpensive, great gifts at your local toy store. It would surely please them because there is so much there that they would love to have and so many things are not terribly expensive.

Stores like Target, K Mart, Wal-Mart and your favorite toy store have a lot of gifts at a reasonable price.

Fabulous Cakes
for a Fraction of the Cost

Remember the cakes of yesteryear? Traditionally wedding cakes have been white, round, tiered or stacked and pretty tasteless. *How they've changed!* From boring cakes balanced on shaky pedestals and topped with a plastic bride and groom -- to absolute works of art that taste as great as they look. Today, anything goes.

Now we're ready to have some fun! Choosing your wedding cake should not only be fun – but *devilishly* fun. What other opportunity would give you the assignment of sampling cakes and frostings?

Butter cream or Royal? Lemon cream filling or vanilla pastry cream? Square cake or layered? So many cakes – so little time. Here again, you can flip through the pages of bridal magazines to find an elegant (or humorous) cake that strikes your fancy. Look at lots of different ideas before you decide what you want. Visit bakeries or you might also find inspiration at a toy store, in china patterns or from your favorite candies.

Your cake is the centerpiece of the reception. It is a scrumptious dessert as well as part of a tradition, the beautiful or messy cutting-of-the-cake.

Your wedding cake says who you are. It can be any shape, color and flavor. Opt for any theme or decoration that suits you. Put some thought and creativity into your wedding and groom cakes to show how you, as a couple, live and think.

What kind of cake will you choose?

❖ Flavors-Choosing the best flavor is personal. If you're going to put extra dollars into your cake, put them into the taste. The main taste of the cake comes from the fillings and frostings. With cake fillings, the sky's the limit on these delectable concoctions -- from traditional custards and cream fillings to exotic liqueurs and fruit. Of course, the more non-traditional the filling, the more cost it will add to your cake. The cake itself can be chocolate, strawberry, carrot cake or cheesecake. You can mix and match red velvet with pistachio. Of course there is always vanilla. Be sure that your fillings and frostings fit the climate. Don't choose a frosting that melts in hot weather if you're having an outdoor summer wedding. And then there's fondant. Some people love it and some people don't. It has a certain look and is also less delicate than butter cream frosting. As for taste, fondant is really not used for flavor. It is used for decoration and to seal in the cake moistness. If you are set on using fondant try the Marshmallow Fondant Recipe at the end of this chapter. It is easy to make and tastes better than traditional fondant.

Tasting the flavors and combinations is one of the best parts of deciding on your wedding cake. Your wedding guests will remember the taste of the cake for a long time and will savor the effort you put into your choices.

Themes-Follow your idea for a theme or color scheme. If you are having a theme or color scheme for your wedding, it would be great to incorporate that onto your cake.

❖ **Decorations**- Ideas for cake decorations are endless.

1. Candy makes for beautiful cake designs. You can use M&M's, Candy canes, Peppermints, Chocolates, Licorice, Mints, Lifesavers, Jolly Ranchers or any other pretty candies. Try all different types of white candies for spectacular white-on-white cake designs.

2. Fruit is also a creative method to use for decoration. Sugared fruit is a classic favorite. It makes even the simplest wedding cake designs exquisite.

HOW TO Sugar Fruit:

Use pasteurized egg whites found in cartons in the dairy section of the supermarket.

Beat the egg whites until bubbles start to form.

Paint fruit with a pastry brush dipped in the whites.

Sprinkle fine sugar on fruit with a sieve or roll fruit in fine sugar. (You can grind regular sugar in a blender until fine).

Let dry completely on a cookie sheet or something similar before using.

Some suitable fruits are: grapes, figs, crabapples, lemons, pears, limes, small apples or cherries.

3. Ribbons to match your color scheme look very elegant. A beautiful silk, wired ribbon, artfully draped around the cake is an excellent and inexpensive choice for cake décor.

4. No doubt chocolate curls would be delicious and pretty.

5. Christmas ornaments make a beautiful Winter Wonderland.

6. Seashells and starfish and sea glass make a stunning beach themed cake.

7. Simple strings of faux pearls draped around the cake make an elegant statement.

8. Flowers- Edible flowers are simple and elegant. Nasturtiums have a peppery taste. Roses have a mild, sweet taste. Lavender is a bit "perfumey". Chicory is spicy and bitter tasting. Oregano is a bit spicy and Pansy has a semi-sweet taste. You can use non-edible flowers, just be sure the flowers are safe, non-poisonous and free of pesticides. An elegant Stargazer Lily on the top tier of your cake, with smaller flowers and greenery cascading down the other layers can be a striking and less costly substitute to cake decorations that take hours for your baker to create. Make a small bouquet and use as a cake topper. Or sprinkle petals, cascading down tiers. Or place flowers around the base of the cake. It's simple and elegant. It's best to pick the flowers the day of the wedding. If that's not possible, store them (except for chicory) on a plate with some water in your fridge.

9. Sentimental or specialty items – If you have a unique figurine or other item that is a symbol of your love for each other, consider using it to decorate the cake. Silk craft items such as butterflies or dragonflies can also be artistically arranged on your cake.

    That's just a few simple decoration ideas to get you started. Think about what you like and incorporate that into your cake design. Wedding cake designs don't have to be expensive to be elegant. Remember, the decorations that adorn your cake should reflect your personalities or beliefs for you, as a couple – not some Hollywood version of what your wedding cake should be.

Where will you get your Cake?

Now is also the time when having a grandmother, aunt, mom or friend whose hobby is cake decorating can be a boon to your budget. But even if you're not one of the lucky ones to have been born in to a cake-decorating family, you shouldn't have any problem finding the cake that suits you – and your budget.

- ❀ **Bakery-** Picking the right bakery and negotiating prices is key. Go to your local bakery. Bring pictures of design ideas. Taste different flavors. Discuss when you need to order, prices and deposits. Don't be afraid to negotiate and get a contract.

- ❀ **Culinary Schools-** Enlisting a culinary school student can be a great way to save money. To find a student baker, Google Culinary Schools in your area. Contact the school and see if they meet your requirements.

- ❀ **Grocery Store –**Grocery stores offer fabulous wedding cakes on the cheap. Many supermarkets and warehouse clubs offer master bakers that do a super job on your wedding cake. They're usually inexpensive and as tasty as any other baker could produce. You can also order plain frosted cakes (not mentioning the word "wedding") and save even more by decorating it yourself. No one will believe that your elegant and delicious cake came from a supermarket.

- ❀ **DIY-**You can do it yourself. Don't be intimidated. Enlist the help of family or friends. You can make it from a cake mix or a favorite recipe. This will save you a bundle of money and it will taste delicious.

Different Ways to do a Wedding Cake:

- ❀ **Fake Cakes-**Fake cakes are big money savers. Enlist the help of an "impersonator." An impersonator, or dummy, cake can be a great cost saver. It's used simply for presentation. The actual cakes that are cut for you and your guests are kept behind the scenes. The dummy cake can be an actual cake – small and elaborately decorated – that you cut for the photo op and is then taken back to the kitchen where other, less elaborate cakes (sheet cakes) are cut and served to the masses. An impersonator cake can also be crafted of Styrofoam, covered with actual frosting for display purposes only. Dummy cakes are a great way to save money and still get the taste of the cake you really want. This is something you can ask about at your bakery or a project that you can do yourself.

♣ **Cupcakes**-Cupcakes are cheap and chic. Cupcakes displayed in round tiers like a cake are very popular as well as cheap and practical. Beautiful adornments include fresh flowers, fruit, ribbon or marzipan sculpted into flowers and figurines. Cupcake Wedding Cakes are the best thing since sliced bread and sliced cake. They are inexpensive, easy to make and easy to make the exact amount you need (one cupcake per person). Baking cups/cupcake liners (available at the supermarket) come in lots of colors including silver and gold. There are even liners that are sheer. The color of cupcake liners adds to the decorations.

Cupcakes may be decorated in lots of pretty ways:

❀Ribbons to match your color scheme look very elegant

❀Flowers of course are beautiful to use on the cupcake wedding cake. A large flower in the middle cupcake would be very chic

❀A beautiful seashell on each cupcake would be perfect for a beach wedding

❀Heart shaped lollipops stuck in each cake is a terrific for a Valentine's Day wedding

❀ Pre-made ribbons atop the cakes are pretty. Don't remove the paper from the sticky tab

❀ All sorts of candy, such as silver Dragees (small sugar balls covered with edible silver leaf) may be used. Use what is appropriate for your theme.

❁ Betty Crocker has an edible pen that writes on cakes

❁ No doubt chocolate curls would be delicious and pretty

❁ Miniature pinwheels, cocktail umbrellas or mini bride and groom figures are some fun things to use

❁ For a Christmas wedding use tiny Christmas trees or ornaments

❁ You could get very creative with a combination of any of these the ideas mentioned

❁ One good idea is to monogram each cupcake with the couple's initials. Use an edible pen or pastry bag to write with

❁ Use three tiered dishes to arrange the cupcake wedding cake

❁ Bake cupcakes in a non-stick pan with NO liners. There will be no crumbs and you can ice the whole cupcake like a miniature cake.

❁ Here's the best one. Arrange all the cupcakes in a rectangle or circle and cover the top with frosting as though it is one cake. Then decorate anyway you like. Each guest can pull off a cupcake.

✿ **Individual Cakes**-Set a small cake at each place setting and individual cakes serve as a favor and as the perfect dessert. You can purchase small cake pans at a craft or kitchen store. Bake one for each guest and there's no slicing or serving. You can make a slightly lager cake for the Head Table and still do the cutting-of-the-cake-ceremony.

✿ **Centerpiece Cakes**-Dual purpose cakes are fun and economical. Make a smaller wedding cake "centerpiece" for each guest table. You can decorate each one differently or keep them in line with your theme. You can even mix up the flavors. Each smaller cake takes the place of more expensive floral centerpieces. Plus it serves as the wedding cake. It is a great way to save money.

Wedding Cake Toppers

Anything can be used as wedding cake toppers. Of course there is the traditional bride and groom but you see many other things now. However if you want the bride and groom they are available. There are lots of choices online and in stores.

You can pick a cake topper that goes along with the theme of your wedding. Toppers should speak to your style.

Some ideas are:

❀ For a fall wedding use mini pumpkins on top with silk maple leaves.

❀ Hibiscus for a tropical wedding is pretty. They only last for a day, so wait until the last minute and lay about three big Hibiscuses on top of the cake.

❀ If you can find a pineapple small enough or are able to find a suitable fake one, that would be a great cake topper for a Hawaiian wedding. You could also add lei around the cake.

❀ Try a dripless candle for a wedding cake topper. A smaller pillar candle would be nice or any candle that's not too heavy. Try putting skewers (found at the super market) around it to hold it up. Push the skewers down into the cake but leave enough sticking out of the cake to hold the candle up. Surround the candle with flowers or ribbons to hide the skewers.

❀ Ribbons are always pretty as a wedding cake topper. Also a big tulle bow with a flower or a wedding bell in the middle is beautiful.

- A Styrofoam ball covered with real or artificial flowers of your choice is a great topper. Cut the flowers down very short and attach a pick with wire. Cover the ball so that none of the Styrofoam is showing. Also use Styrofoam cut into different shapes, such as a heart.

- Mickey and Minnie Mouse on top of the cake is fun. If you are going to Disney World for your honeymoon this would tie right in. If you just love Mickey and Minnie it is great too.

- Anything that the couple has a big interest in could be used, such as a toy motorcycle, etc. Shop around for toys or trinkets that would be suitable.

- Barbie and Ken dolls are a good wedding cake topper. Any similar dolls would work as well.

- A Christmas wedding just screams for a Santa wedding cake topper. Also use clear plastic ornaments filled with flower petals. Wire them to a skewer and arrange on the cake. You could also use silk poinsettias as well (never use the real thing, they're poisonous)!

Let your imagination run wild and come up with your own unique wedding cake topper.

Groom's Cakes

Having a grooms cake is a tradition that has come and gone and is making somewhat of a comeback. This special cake for the groom is thought to have started in the South. It began as a second cake presented at the reception, with a heavier recipe and sometimes soaked with liquor.

Legend says that unmarried girls would take a piece home and sleep with it under their pillows to help them dream of the man they would marry. Well, times have changed. The best part of this tradition is that the groom has something special for him. There are so many options today.

Great Grooms Cake tips:

❀ Originally, the cake was served at the reception alongside the wedding cake. Today, some serve it at the rehearsal dinner.

❀ Either the bride OR the groom can pick out the design and surprise the other to make it fun.

❀ Choose a design that says something about a special interest or hobby of the groom.

❀ Have a special person in your life make the groom's wedding cake. His mom or the bride's mom would add a personal touch.

❀ Does the groom have a favorite junk-food snack? Pile several donuts, snack cakes, cookies or any other sweets onto pretty cake plates.

❀ 3-D is pretty popular. Think 3-D sports equipment shaped cakes. Think 3-D cars, trucks, briefcases, TV sets and remotes.

If you are really strapped for cash...skip the Groom's cake altogether. If you decide to have one, probably the best way to save money here is to either get help making the cake or get a local baker to cut you a deal for both cakes. Any way you "slice" it; groom cakes are a cool way to make the groom feel special.

More on Cutting Cake Corners

Aside from having a friend or relative (or yourself) bake and decorate your wedding cake, visit a bakery that you're already familiar with or that comes with a great recommendation from someone you know. Some bakeries may give you a special discount if they cater to you and your family on a regular basis.

A stacked, three of four-tiered cake with plain frosting is much less expensive than one that requires separators and columns. You can always add the decorations after you receive the cake.

Don't bother with a dessert table as part of the wedding reception menu if you're planning to serve wedding cake. It's an unnecessary expense that you don't need if you're on a budget.

Any delectable dessert that you can imagine can be made into a "wedding cake." Some brides are choosing cheesecakes, others choose Twinkies or chocolates. One recent bride even had a cake fashioned from Krispy Kreme Donuts.

Have someone pick up the cake rather than pay a delivery fee. Be sure and speak to the baker about the proper way to transport the cake to keep it from tilting or sliding into a disastrous mess.

It's best not to order your cake from a bridal salon and risk hidden or exorbitant fees. Also, when it comes to purchasing a cake knife, try to find a plain one and decorate it yourself with fanciful ribbon.

Watch out for cake cutting fees that can add up in a hurry. Ask the caterer or manager beforehand what his or her policy is for cutting the cake. If they charge for it, negotiate with them or offer to cut the cake yourself and then enlist the help of a friend or family member.

Keep your wedding cake needs fun and simple. There are so many choices available that will be pleasing to both the eye and the palate - and save you money besides. The possibilities are endless when it comes to having a marvelous confection that will long be remembered after it's eaten and smashed in the face of the bride and groom.

BONUS RECIPIE:

Marshmallow Fondant Recipe:

You can use marshmallow fondant as you would regular fondant, to cover cakes, form shapes, and make candy. Beware it tends to get sticky in moist places, so it doesn't hold up as well as regular fondant when placed over frosting and refrigerated for days. This recipe makes 1.5 lbs of fondant, and can easily be doubled or halved.

Ingredients:

- ❀ 8 ounces miniature marshmallows (4 cups not packed, or half of a 16-ounce bag)

- 1 pound powdered sugar (4 cups), plus extra for dusting
- Flavored extracts or food coloring (optional)
- 2 tbsp water
- ¼ cup Crisco shortening

Preparation:

Place the Crisco in a shallow bowl and set aside.

Dust your work surface with powdered sugar. Put the marshmallows and the water in a large microwave-safe bowl. Microwave marshmallows on high for 1 minute, until they have expanded and are puffy.

Stir the marshmallows with a rubber spatula until they're melted and smooth. If some unmelted marshmallow bits remain, place back in the microwave for 30-45 seconds, until the marshmallow mixture is entirely smooth and free of lumps. If you want colored or flavored fondant, you can add several drops of food coloring or extracts now and stir until well incorporated. NOTE: If you want to create multiple colors or flavors from one batch of fondant, do not add the colors or flavors now. Instead, see step 7 below for instructions.

Add the powdered sugar and begin to stir with the spatula. Stir until the sugar begins to incorporate and it becomes impossible to stir anymore.

Scrape the marshmallow-sugar mixture out onto the prepared work surface. It will be sticky and lumpy, with lots of sugar that has not been incorporated yet--this is okay. Rub your hands in the Crisco thoroughly, and start to knead the fondant mixture like bread dough, working the sugar into the marshmallow with your hands.

Continue to knead the fondant until it smoothes out and loses its stickiness. Add more sugar if necessary, but be careful and stop adding sugar once it is smooth--too much sugar will make it stiff and hard to work with. Once the fondant is a smooth ball, it is ready to be used. You can now roll it out, shape it, or wrap it in cling wrap to use later. Well-wrapped fondant can be stored in a cool room or in the refrigerator. It needs to be kneaded until supple before later use.

If you want to add several different colorings or flavorings to your fondant, flatten it into a round disc. You might want to wear gloves to avoid getting food coloring on your hands during this step. Add the desired amount of coloring or flavoring to the center of the disc, and fold the disc over on itself so that the color or flavor is enclosed in the center of the fondant ball.

Begin to knead the ball of fondant just like you did before. As you work it, you will begin to see streaks of color coming through from the center. Knead until the streaks are gone and the fondant is uniform in color. Your fondant is now ready to be used or stored as mentioned above.

Savings on Every Element of Your Ceremony

There are many ways to have a beautiful wedding ceremony. Since you have decided early on in the planning process where the ceremony will be held, now you just have to decide how you want your ceremony to look and what elements you would like to include.

These are typical elements of a wedding ceremony:

➤ Wedding Processional.

➤ Music and Wedding Readings.

➤ Wedding Vows.

➤ Exchange of Wedding Rings.

➤ Officiant's sanction of the marriage.

➤ A first kiss as a married couple.

➤ A Recessional.

➤ Witnesses to sign the marriage license.

A ceremony might also include a unity candle ceremony, a rose ceremony or any other religious ritual or family tradition.

The perfect ceremony is the one from your heart. Do what is right for you and your fiancée. If you can imagine your dream ceremony, you can create it.

A great way to save money on your ceremony overall is to combine the site of the ceremony and reception. Just be sure to compare prices on all the elements. You just may save time and money by combining decorations, flowers, photography, music and various other rentals.

Likely the cheapest ceremony of all would be to get married in a civil ceremony at your local courthouse/city hall with just a few in attendance, then spend your budget on the reception.

Officiant

Finding the right wedding Officiant to marry you is an important choice. You want someone who is in alignment with your beliefs and who understands your style. They also help create the tone and feel of the ceremony.

Here are some questions to think about when looking for the right Officiant for your ceremony:

✔ Does their personality jive with yours?

✔ Do they have a clear, pleasant speaking voice?

✔ Will they charge extra for attending the rehearsal?

✔ Do you want to write your own vows or will you leave up to the Officiant?

Many people are going the DIY Officiant route. Having a friend or family member marry you and your fiancée is becoming increasingly popular.

You might be lucky enough to live in a state where laypeople are allowed to officiate at civil wedding ceremonies. Usually, the would-be Officiant has to file some paperwork and pay a small fee a few weeks or months before the wedding. Then the person is granted a temporary title that allows them to perform one wedding. It is good for only one day. Check to see if this is available in your state.

The other option is to have your friend or family member become an ordained clergyperson.

There are a few religious associations that will ordain anyone online, instantly for FREE! The Universal Life Church is one such organization.

Once your friend is ordained they may be required to register with your state or county as a religious Officiant who can perform weddings. This whole process may take some time so make sure your would-be-Officiant starts the process at least two months ahead of time.

Programs

Wedding programs add an extra special touch to your big day. But do you really need a wedding program? If money is tight or you're short on time, skip the programs.

For certain ceremonies they are more important than others. For example, if your ceremony is going to be long, it will help your guests follow along and know what to expect.

Or if you are having a traditional or religious wedding and many of your guests are of another culture or faith. It's also a good idea to have a program if you have a lot of people you would like to thank.

If you want to have programs and save cash you might want to consider making them using template designs from a computer program. Or you can buy a DIY kit from craft stores or online sites. Just follow the directions and put the programs together.

You can even create programs yourself them from scratch.

Program Materials:

- ❁ Quality paper   ❁ Printer   ❁ Hole Punch
- ❁ Ribbon   ❁ Scissors

With your Microsoft Word program or any other art project program, and some help from friends, you can easily and economically have beautiful programs that your guests will cherish as keepsakes.

Tips on things you can include in your programs:

- ❁ Use any type stationery you like. The program can be one side of one card, or as large as a booklet.
- ❁ Include notes on why certain music selections were chosen.
- ❁ Explain what particular religious or cultural parts of the ceremony mean.
- ❁ When listing the wedding party, make sure to include how each person is related to the bride or groom. (e.g. Susie Smith, bride's cousin).
- ❁ Include favorite poetry or song lyrics.
- ❁ This is the perfect place to incorporate your theme and/or colors.
- ❁ Include quotes from the bride and groom.
- ❁ Take the opportunity to thank everyone for sharing this most special day.
- ❁ Include a digital photo of the couple.

Offering a wedding program to guests allows them to fully experience what is going on during the ceremony and provides guests with a lovely keepsake.

Music

A formal wedding is a time for joy and inspiration. You may get by with an organist or pianist that plays beautiful, reflective music, as the guests are seated and more triumphant melodies when the ceremony ends and the new couple is introduced.

Here are some helpful hints for saving money on the music for your ceremony:

If you're having the ceremony in a house of worship, inquire about getting free musicians, organist or singer(s). Being a member of the house of worship makes it easier and more likely that they will provide you with free music – or music at a lesser cost. You might want to offer a donation if it's within your budget.

Call an alma mater and ask what their policy is for letting students sing or play at wedding ceremonies. You may be able to get a high school or community choir to sing for free – just for the practice.

Music from a digital source like an iPod is a great way to get a flawless performance – and to have exactly what you want. Pay attention to the acoustics to be sure the sound is what you want it to be.

Do you have a talented friend or family member? Ask them to sing or perform at your ceremony!

Have a single guitarist play for your ceremony. You can find many talented players at high schools, music schools and local clubs.

A harpist creates a beautiful sound for a wedding ceremony and can sometimes be the least expensive form of available music.

Combine instruments such as a flute and a violin to create a beautiful sound for your ceremony.

It's important to set the mood for your ceremony, but remember that the actual ceremony usually only lasts for a few minutes. Don't blow your budget here – keep the big bucks for the reception.

Decorating

Wedding decorations add so much to the ceremony. They set the mood and ambiance.

Although, decorating for the ceremony is a little different than doing so for the reception. Sometimes the location may not need any further decorations or certain things may not be allowed. Check with your church or venue first.

There are special spots at the wedding ceremony that call for attention.

Places to Adorn:

- ❀ Entrance or the doorway
- ❀ Arches
- ❀ Trellises
- ❀ Tents
- ❀ Pews
- ❀ Chairs
- ❀ Altar

Entrance or Doorway:

Topiaries are perfect for entrances or doorways. You can buy them at your local garden center or you can make them yourself. For easy directions on how to make a topiary go to http://www.cheap-chic-weddings.com/wedding-reception-decorations.html

Garlands made from flowers (real or fake), paper or ribbon makes an outstanding entrance or doorway decoration. Floral sprays work very well too.

Arches and Trellises:

If you are having an outdoor wedding there may be an arch or a trellis involved. The easy way to decorate an arch is with artificial flowers attached to the arch with plastic cable ties purchased at your hardware store.

It's easy because you don't have to worry about keeping them alive and they can be done the day before. Just arrange in a fashion that hides the plastic ties. Use flowers that are the same type that you are using in your wedding. You may use tulle or ribbon in conjunction with the flowers.

A trellis can be decorated pretty much the same as an arch. Just weave some tulle through the trellis and attach some flowers. Pick silk flowers that look as real as possible. There are some gorgeous ones out there. Adding silk greenery is an inexpensive way to add filler to make the flowers go a long way.

Tents:
The best decorations for a tent are lighting. Consider using spotlights as well as Holiday Lights as they go a long way in creating mood pretty inexpensively. Lanterns add a magical feel also. Tulle or chiffon in classic white or your wedding colors can add drama as well. You can also bring in natural elements like flowers, greenery and branches.

Pews and Chair:
Paper cones made from pretty craft paper can be hung with ribbon from pews or chair backs. You can fill them with baby's breath, dried or silk flowers...no wire or water required. This is perfect for church, as you don't want to have water damage or scratches on the pews. You can also add these to chairs.

Hang a small, framed sign of the bride's initials on the pews for the bride's family. Do the same with the groom's initials for his family's side. You could hot glue a pretty ribbon, flower or both to adorn.

Pomanders made using faux flowers and Styrofoam are elegant for pews and chairs. See http://www.cheap-chic-weddings.com/wedding-flowers.html for simple instructions.

Altar:
Depending on where your ceremony takes place you may use flower arrangements, potted plants, garlands, wreaths or topiaries. Your location will dictate what the decorations should be.

Incorporating different materials into the décor can save you money and time. Consider bows, tulle, candles and paper.

Floral Arrangements
Flowers are the most common decorations for wedding ceremonies. Unfortunately, floral arrangements can be very expensive.

Here are a few money saving tips:

Buy your flowers from a wholesale online florist. Many of them sell pre-made wedding packages. You can choose the color, type and quantity. Engage your family and friends to help you prepare them for your ceremony. Many of these web sites offer helpful advice on how to keep your flowers pretty and fresh.

Skip the florist and go straight to the supermarket. Many of them offer full service on all your floral needs at a much lower price.

Consider using silk or faux flowers. Sometimes they can be cheaper, depending on where you buy them and if they are on sale.

See Chapter 7 for more great ideas on flowers and saving money.

Don't Blow the Budget on the Reception

A wedding reception is when a bride and groom are introduced for the first time as a married couple. The hosts often throw a party with food, drink and music to celebrate the big day.

It is traditional to entertain guests after a wedding ceremony. The party can be simple or elaborate. It can last for an hour or even days. Of course you want it to be nice and you want everyone to enjoy it. The party should reflect the style and spirit of the wedding but you don't want to spend a fortune. There are a lot of creative solutions to saving money at your wedding reception.

Location

If you book your reception at a hall, hotel ballroom or restaurant, the catering manager can act as a wedding coordinator, saving you big money and time. They can provide services such as cakes, a D.J. and florists at reasonable prices. It's like one-stop shopping.

When comparing the cost of different locations, remember rental fee, food, beverages, parking, gratuity, set-up fees and the cost of rentals like tables, chairs, canopies, etc.

TIP: Don't forget that if your reception is outside to have a back-up plan.

Get everything in writing. Check over the contracts carefully and don't be afraid to negotiate.

Food

Your wedding reception food budget dictates the size of your wedding reception so keep it small to save money. The most obvious way is to limit the number of guests you invite to the wedding.

The time of day that you serve wedding reception food can save you a lot of money. It will also cost you less if you're willing to use some elbow grease and do it yourself. Of course, you can ask for help from your family and attendants.

Here are some common times of day to have a wedding reception and some wedding reception food ideas:

- ❀ A brunch reception would take place at 10 or 11 a.m. It is quite inexpensive because fruit, bread, muffins, mimosas and other breakfast foods would be served. Of course you would have to get ready very, very early.

- ❀ Consider a buffet or do-it-yourself, with help of course.

- ❀ A luncheon reception follows a late morning wedding. You can easily make this food yourself as it is made up of sandwiches (finger sandwiches are nice), green salad, pasta salad and fruit. You can put a tray of cold cuts together and garnish it nicely and it would be great.

- ❀ The dessert reception is the most inexpensive wedding reception food. It's great if you do have a lot of people and not much money. The menu is self-explanatory. Just serve your favorite desserts made by you or family members. This type of reception could be held at 9 or 10 p.m., after dinner hours. That means the ceremony will be for no earlier than 8 p.m. Just mention on the wedding invitations that you are having a dessert reception so guests will know to eat dinner beforehand.

- ❀ The cocktail party reception is less expensive than dinner and is held from 4 to 7 p.m. Serve just hors d'oeuvres (made by you). Supermarkets offer hors d'oeuvres trays pretty inexpensively also. Redo them with your own garnish and make them really pretty.

- ❀ Then there's the dinner reception, the most expensive. You can still save though by doing it yourself. Or serve it buffet style and make a nice presentation. You can also order maybe just the entrée from your favorite restaurant and make the rest yourself. It wouldn't be too expensive if you picked it up and set it up yourself.

- ❀ If you're having a very informal wedding do a barbecue at your home or in a park or on the beach for your wedding reception food. You could do any of the above at your home as well. If you're having a church wedding, have a luncheon or dessert reception in the church hall.

TIP: If you are using a caterer, keep it simple and don't be afraid to put a halt to anything you see as an added expense that you'd rather not have. Most caterers will work with you and your budget to give the most detail for your dollars. Be sure to get references and check him or her out as much as you can. When the time comes to make a deposit, it's best to use a credit card rather than non-refundable cash.

Here Are a Few More Money Saving Ideas:

- ❧ Choose Exotic and Inexpensive Ethnic Foods – Great money-saving ethnic menus can be found if you're open to serving Chinese, Mexican, Greek and Middle-Eastern menus.

- ❧ Kebabs are Cheaper than Steaks – You can make very little meat go a long way by inserting veggie bites between the meat, and it makes a very appealing visual impact.

- ❧ Choose Seasonal – Tell your caterer to keep the costs down by choosing seasonal vegetables and other items. They'll also be fresher!

- ❧ Forget the Caterer – Plan a Coordinated Potluck. If you're watching every penny, you may want to enlist the help of friends and family to provide the reception menu – especially if you have access to some talented cooks.

- ❧ Shop for Appetizers at Bulk Discount Stores -- Stores such as Sam's Club and Costco offer bulk items at wholesale prices. You can also find inexpensive party platters, beautifully arranged.

- ❧ Dessert-Only – Many couples today are opting to serve champagne along with the wedding cake and other desserts. This will save you a bucketful of money that you can put to better use.

- ❧ All Inclusive Wedding – If you choose a destination wedding or another type of all-inclusive style wedding, the cake, drinks and food should be included in the price. It's also a good way to avoid the fuss of planning.

Whatever you decide to do for your wedding reception food, do it for less without the stress.

Drinks

Alcoholic beverages are a big part of any wedding reception – and also one of the most expensive. If you choose to have an open bar during the reception, it could run into thousands of dollars – something you want to avoid if you're on a tight budget.

On top of the price of liquor, champagne and wine you might incur a corking fee, serving fees and gratuity. And don't be surprised if you're charged for liquor that you didn't even use.

As a bride planning your own wedding, you'll need the following tips before you decide on the liquor needs for your wedding reception:

- ❀ You can save over 50% on liquor by buying your own at discount mega stores like Sam's Club or Costco. If you let the reception site provide the liquor, you could face more than double the wholesale price!

- ❀ Don't let your caterer purchase the alcohol! You're in for spending more money if you do.

- ❀ Check with any store where you buy liquor to see if you can get a refund on unopened bottles and if they offer case discounts.

- ❀ Tell the servers that you only want the wine or liquor opened as needed, rather than opened all at the same time.

- ❀ Don't choose champagne fountains! They're very expensive, and guests have a tendency to over drink. If you must have a fountain, they can be filled with an inexpensive non-alcoholic beverage.

- ❀ Rather than having an open bar, choose to serve a combination of house wines (red, white and sparkling), beer and some non-alcoholic beverages such as coffee and punch.

- ❀ Go completely non-alcoholic and serve some delightful alternatives such as a creative punch bowl or fountain, smoothies or sodas.

If you must have champagne, bring it out only for a toast to the bride and groom.

Liquor and wine can account for an enormous portion of your wedding menu budget. Be a smart bride and determine where you're going to cut costs before you shop.

Do's and Don'ts for Wedding Receptions

Every bride wants to please her wedding guests by offering a unique and exquisite menu at the reception. That wish can be accomplished by following the tips in this chapter.

There are some other factors to consider when planning your reception menu that will go a long way to making it a huge success and one that your guests will fondly remember for a long time.

For example:

❀ Never have your guests pay for their own drinks. Find other ways to cut liquor and wine expenses.

❀ Be sure that the quality of the food served is top-notch. You may want to skimp on another portion of your budget to be sure that you're getting top quality – but it's worth the effort.

❀ If your bartender places a tip jar on the bar, insist they remove it. You're probably being charged for gratuities anyway. Don't make your guests pay extra.

❀ Before the reception, check out the kitchen and bathroom facilities. Make sure they're clean and that everything needed is provided.

❀ Insist on having a taste test before you finalize the venue for your reception. If the food isn't good, you'll be paying for uneaten meals. You might want to test one more time before the reception takes place.

❀ Be sure there'll be enough food. Ask your caterer or server about a "guaranteed minimum." This ensures that if you've invited (for example) 125 guests and only 100 attend, you won't be charged for the other 25.

❀ You don't have to offer numerous choices, but do take into consideration that many of your guests may not like unusual or exotic foods. Offer a veggie tray as an alternative.

Remember that the reception is supposed to be a celebration of your unity as a couple. As long as you've created memorable ways for your guests to participate in your marriage celebration – the food and drink will be secondary.

Decorations

Get creative with wedding decorations. Wedding reception decorations are fun. Themes can dictate what they will be if you are going that route.

Here are some general ideas:

❀ If there are potted plants or trees in the room, decorate them with strings of white lights. These plants can be purchased pretty cheaply at your local home improvement center or nursery. After using them for your wedding reception decorations, you can use them at your home.

❀ Tablecloths and napkins can add a lot to the reception decorations. For napkin rings glue a silk flower to a ribbon and tie onto napkin. The rings may also be made of wire and beads. Make a hook at one end of wire. Wrap around a napkin to get the correct size. Put beads on and make a hook at the remaining end. Hook together.

❀ Balloons are a beautiful and economical way to decorate your wedding. They are fairly simple to create yourself. Balloons are a fun way to turn your reception venue into a fairyland.

Here are several designs to consider:

Balloon arches	Columns
Topiaries	Flowers
Bouquets	Centerpieces
"String of Pearls"	

There are also balloons that can burst into a confetti shower.

You can choose balloons with sparkling lights that can be strung around the room to give a festive ambiance.

Check online for balloon companies, kits and how-to directions.

❀ Lighting can add so much to your reception site and really set the mood. You can use Christmas lights, up lights, Gobos, Luminaries.

❀ Topiaries are wonderful for wedding reception decorations, side tables or sitting on the floor.

You will need:

A pot for the size topiary you need
Correct size Styrofoam ball
Floral foam
Small tree limb or dowel
Silk flowers
Moss
Glue gun and glue sticks
Ribbon

HOW TO: Cut floral foam to fit snugly into pot and secure with hot glue. Place limb or dowel into floral foam and make sure it's secure with glue. Place the Styrofoam ball onto limb or dowel with hot glue. Cut flowers to about 2 or 3 inches long. Insert the flowers and greenery into the Styrofoam making sure they all stick out evenly. Tie bows with the ribbon and pin onto ball in between flowers. Use anything you would like to include in the topiary. If you have used a dowel wrap it with ribbon. If a limb was used you can just leave it as is.

❀ A flower ball may be made with a Styrofoam ball, silk flowers and ribbon. Insert flowers into ball until completely covered. Glue a ribbon bow to the center. Cut ribbon to the desired length for a hanger and attach to the Styrofoam with one or two pins. Glue it as well to make sure it's secure.

❀ Tie big tulle bows around the backs of chairs. Flowers can be attached to bows with wire or glue.

❀ Make a candle wedding reception decoration with:

> Clear Christmas balls
> Clear curtain rings
> Desired platter or plate
> Epsom salt
> Candles to fit into ornament openings
>
> **HOW TO:** Remove hangers from ornaments. Arrange the curtain rings on the platter. Pour Epsom salt into each ornament, filling halfway to the top. Place the ornaments on top of the curtain rings. Place candles into the openings of the ornaments, pressing into the Epsom salt to secure. Arrange greenery or whatever you like around the candles. You may use colored sand if you like.

❀ If the wedding is near a particular holiday, such as Christmas, use wedding reception decorations appropriate for that season. That makes it real easy. Big bowls of Christmas ornaments are elegant.

❀ Goldfish bowls with a real goldfish in it are a good wedding reception decoration idea. A few flowers or candles around it would be pretty. Put aquarium rocks in the bowl in your color.

❀ Candles can be made from sheets of beeswax purchased at the craft store. Use a cookie cuter in the shape of a wedding bell and cut six or more if you want them thicker. Heat wax slightly with a hair dryer to stick one half together. Place a wick inside and stick the other half on.

❀ Instead of putting the favors at each place, you could put them in one big container in the center of the table. That would eliminate using flowers. If they are tied with ribbons just don't crush the bows or any other decoration that is on them.

Wedding reception decorations only call for your imagination.

Centerpieces

Wedding centerpieces can be very inexpensive. The following ideas include flowers and materials that aren't flowers but that add a lot to centerpiece ideas.

Here are some suggestions that will stir your imagination:

❀ Large bouquets can be made with big bunches of Baby's Breath only. It looks high end if it is large and makes a beautiful statement. For the head table you can do the same thing but add a few roses.

❀ If you have a gardenia bush that is in bloom when you're having your wedding, they would be outstanding floating in a pedestal bowl. Tie a satin ribbon around the pedestal. Use a color that coordinates with your wedding. Camellias are gorgeous used this way and make great wedding centerpieces. Oh, by the way, don't touch your gardenia petals or they will turn yellow.

❀ Fruit is inexpensive and can be made into lovely wedding centerpieces. Try to find fruit that isn't blemished. Stack it pyramid style in a glass bowl or on a pedestal glass stand. Frosted fruit makes a wonderful wedding centerpiece. Some fruits to use are; strawberries, figs, apricots, pears, plums, grapes, oranges, lemons, limes, apples, any berries, cherries, kumquats, cranberries and pomegranates that have been cut in half to show the beautiful seeds.

HOW TO: Use pasteurized egg whites found in cartons in the dairy section of the supermarket. Beat the egg whites until bubbles start to form. Paint fruit with a pastry brush dipped in the whites.

Sprinkle fine sugar on fruit with a sieve or roll fruit in sugar. (you can grind up regular sugar in a blender or food processor) Let dry completely on a cookie sheet or something similar before using.

❀ Raw cranberries may be put in a glass bowl and topped with frosted fruit. You can use cranberries in a glass vase also for a flower arrangement.

❀ If you have a bougainvillea bush or know someone who does, they are gorgeous for making wedding centerpieces. They come in many colors and are very showy. Make them in into an upright bouquet or a long arrangement. For that use some sort of shallow dish or plate. Tape an oasis to the dish that has been soaked for a good long time in water. Stick long branches into each end and fill in with shorter ones to hide the oasis.

❀ Hydrangeas, Azaleas, Dogwood blooms and Magnolias from your garden or a friend's, are perfect arranged in any way you like.

❀ Have your friends save glass jars for you of any size. They don't all have to be the same because they will be covered. Measure your containers up both sides, across the bottom and up the other side and add about three inches. Cut circles of tulle these dimensions. Sit your container in the center and gather up around the sides and put a rubber band at the top to hold. Fluff up the top and play with it to hide the rubber band. Put water in your container and fill with flowers.

❀ An extremely cheap wedding centerpiece could be made with branches (with leaves) from your yard or someone else's. Spay paint them with silver or gold or any color you like and arrange them in any container that suits you. They would be nice used with clear Christmas ornaments that have been painted inside.

HOW TO: Take the top off the ornament and pour paint color(s) of your choice inside them and swirl around until you achieve the look you want. With more than one color you will get a marbled look. You may make a long low arrangement in floral foam or a tall one in a vase. You could use them with a few flowers or tulle bows.

- Hibiscus blooms can be put around on a table with no water. They will last for one day. Use them with any other arrangements. Rose petals can be spread on the table also. Get roses that have seen better days and are on sale. Use just the petals.

- Lots of small, pretty containers with one bloom can be used for lovely wedding centerpieces.

- Candles are very nice with any flowers or anything else you are using. Floating candles in a glass bowl with a few floating blooms are exquisite wedding centerpieces. You could even sprinkle a little glitter on top of the water in your color.

- Don't forget potted plants can be used and are very pretty. Caladiums or azaleas or anything with a colorful leaf or bloom works great.

If you feel comfortable doing so, buy the flowers and decorate the site yourself use a friend or family member to help. Lots of bargains can be found at low prices if you're willing to do the footwork.

Wedding centerpieces can be created from just about anything. Use your imagination and have fun doing it.

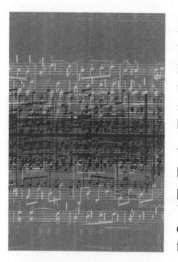

Music

You could have danced all night! Maybe not, if you knew how much it was costing. But with these tips, you should be able to find some great music for your reception without breaking the bank.

The bulk of your music cost will probably be for the reception. This is the arena where people like to eat, drink and be merry – "be merry" meaning that they'll dance to everything from the Funky Chicken to hits from the 40s.

When you're shopping, be sure and find out if the musicians, DJs and singers are available for the date of your wedding. If you're planning a holiday wedding, you might run into some difficulties finding what you want – and if you do, they're likely to be more expensive.

Besides availability, be sure to ask about fees, overtime, travel expenses or mileage and get a contract stating what is expected of them. Now, on to find the music you want for the best possible price.

The reception music sets the tone for the entire evening of celebration. This is what you'll want the emphasis of your music budget to focus on.

The type of music you should have depends entirely on your likes and dislikes as a couple. Don't hire a rousing band or DJ when you'd rather hear Vivaldi playing in the background.

If you're the party-all-night type of couple, you'll want to be sure that you hire a group or individual that will give you the most "renditions" for the buck.

Here are some thoughts that might save you some money when you're shopping for reception entertainment:

- ❀ Don't begin too early – If you're having a seated dinner or hour-long cocktail party, schedule the main entertainment to begin later in the evening. You don't want dancing to begin while your guests are just sitting down to dinner or attempting to chat while the bride and groom are still in their photo session

- ❀ DJs usually charge extra for Saturday nights – Again, when you schedule your wedding is all-important to the money you'll be able to save on music. If you've scheduled your wedding on a day other than Saturday, ask about a discount.

- ❀ Hire the same music group or individual for the ceremony and the reception – Many will give you a discount if you hire them for both events.

- ❀ Don't let them charge for extras – You can avoid extra costs by nixing items such as an assistant for the DJ and light or bubble shows.

- ❀ Get recommendations – Ask newly married couples for recommendations on entertainers. Also, your caterer and other professionals who are working with you to manage your wedding may have names of people or groups who they've worked with in the past.

- A DJ is usually more economical – Especially if you hire him or her for both the ceremony and the reception. A great DJ can get the party going in no time and if they play weddings on a regular basis, they'll have a great repertoire of music.

- Attend Bridal Shows – This is a great way to shop for a DJ or band for your reception. Some hand out free tapes and CDs. They'll also provide price lists and brochures -- and you may get the chance to see them perform live.

- If your wedding and reception are to be held outdoors, be sure you have the use of a good sound system.

The main thing to remember when you're shopping for reception music is to focus on what you, as a couple, would like to hear – and stick to the plan.

Music to Fit Every Budget –
Get It for Less or Get It for FREE!

What most future brides don't know is that they can get the perfect music for the vision of their wedding if they take the time to research.

If you're a bride who is really intent on keeping to a budget, you'll benefit enormously by looking at every option available before you make a decision to pay dearly for your ceremony and reception entertainment.

Below are a few money-saving options for entertainment that you may want to consider before inflating the music portion of your "pie."

- Ask about piped music – It's FREE! You don't want dreary music playing in the background, but if the tunes are uplifting and acceptable – use it rather than hiring someone at an astronomical hourly rate.

- Get a friend or family member to help with music – It's FREE! If you have access to a great selection of CDs or tapes, ask a friend or family member to be your DJ for free. That's what friends are for.

- Check out library CDs – It's FREE! You may be able to find ceremony music and music designed for the cocktail hour and reception tunes for dancing and celebrating

- Hire local musicians or DJ – Hiring local may help you avoid transportation or mileage fees.

- Call a local Senior Citizen's Center – Many active Senior Citizens' Centers have practicing musicians who would be honored to play at your wedding and/or reception for a nominal fee.

- Local Symphony Orchestra – This is a great way to get real talent for your wedding and cut the cost by as much as 50%. Some orchestras have formed small "breakaway" groups that might include a violin and piano that would be perfect music for your wedding.

- Newspapers – Research the society pages of your local newspaper to find groups or individuals who have performed at local events.

When it's all about saving money and working with a tight wedding budget, remember that if you keep everything simple, you'll come much closer to meeting all of your wedding budget goals.

You'll remember the music that was performed at your ceremony and reception for many years to come, so it's one of the most important aspects of your wedding. Think carefully about what you both envision and then set about to get exactly what you want by shopping wisely.

Don't be pushed into having music that you'll both grit your teeth over when you think of it on future anniversaries. It's your wedding – enjoy.

Tipping

Wedding tipping is a detail that should be kept in mind while planning and budgeting your wedding. It will take a lot off your mind if you assign someone to help you out with tipping.

Usually the Best Man or a family member is used to hold the tips and give them out at the appropriate time.

The only way that you'll save money in the wedding tipping department is if you do not use all of these services. If you do use any or all of the following services, then gratuities should be distributed to those who offer good service.

The following is a guideline to the most common wedding tipping:

- ➤ Limousine Drivers – Check your contract to see if it's included, if not then tip 15% - 20%.

- ➤ Coat Rooms – Usually 50 cents to $1.00 per guest. Sometimes you can pre-arrange a flat fee.

- ➤ Judge, Justice of the Peace, or City Clerk – If they do not charge for the ceremony, then $50 - $75 is appropriate. Some charge a fee and cannot accept tips.

- ➤ Clergymen, Rabbis, Priests – No less than $75 - $100. The Best Man traditionally gives after the ceremony.

- ➤ Organist, Musician – This is usually included in the church fee. If not, then tip no less than $35 - $50

- ➤ Florists, Bakers, Photographers – Tip 15% only for extra special service.

- ➤ Parking Attendants - $1 - $2 per car if they are not taking tips from guests.

- ➤ Caterer or Banquet Manager – May be included in your contract. If not, tip 15% - 20%. Extra can be give for exceptional service.

- ➤ Band - $15-20 per band member

- ➤ DJ – 15%- 20% for an exceptional job. Not always required.

- ➤ Bartender – $20-25. May be included in your contract. Give extra only for exceptional service.

Again, you'll save lots of money when any of these services are done by yourself or friends and family. You'll also save tons on wedding tipping by, for example, parking your cars yourself, etc.

Totally Unique Ways to Save Big Money

With a little extra work you can save big money on your wedding. Of course common sense rules here. Start with the traditional ways to cut down expenses like we discussed in the other chapters of this book.

If you are looking for some more ambitious ways to be frugal...here are some "out-of-the-box" ideas.

Negotiating

The skill of negotiating can take you far in life. In the wedding world, it can take you down the aisle...for a lot less money.

Here are tips for foolproof negotiating:

- ✔ Expect the best outcome
- ✔ Don't be scared to ask
- ✔ Be knowledgeable and prepared
- ✔ Be friendly and likable
- ✔ Be quiet and listen.
- ✔ Relax and don't rush
- ✔ Show the other person how you both can win
- ✔ Don't take anything personally
- ✔ Don't give anything away without getting something in return
- ✔ Always be willing to walk away

Bartering

Bartering is simple. You trade something you have for something they have. No money is exchanged.

Do you have a special skill, service or item that you can offer a vendor in exchange for their service or item?

For example, you could swap your graphic design expertise for your wedding flowers. A florist may be looking for new brochures or a website update. It's a win-win situation.

Here are a few tips to keep in mind when making swaps:

- ✔ Make sure what you have to offer has real value
- ✔ Only barter with someone that you would do business with anyway
- ✔ Get the deal in writing

✔ Check with your accountant to see if your exchange affects your taxes

Bartering is gaining popularity, making it easier than ever to find deals. It is definitely something you should consider if you are looking for a way to achieve your dream wedding.

Sponsored Weddings

A sponsored wedding is when a company tastefully advertises at your event. This advertising may include free or discounted services or items for your big day.

Even though celebrities can afford their dream wedding, they have been enjoying sponsored weddings for a long time. You can enjoy the benefits as well. This is a great way to have your dream wedding without going broke.

Be forewarned...some people think having a sponsored wedding is tacky. Think about it though...it is done everyday in different ways. Individuals get ads wrapped on their cars and in exchange get money or a free car. Little League sports teams get sponsors for uniforms, young skateboarders get sponsors to enter competitions and racecar teams have numerous sponsors. If you don't feel comfortable with it don't do it.

You can also choose to try and get everything sponsored or just certain things sponsored like the cake or just flowers. Do what is comfortable for you and your guests.

Here are some tips to make it happen:

✔ Make a list of what you want for your wedding
✔ Make a list of potential sponsors
✔ Decide what you are going to provide to the sponsor (I.e. ads on your wedding website, place cards, verbal thank you etc.)
✔ Think creatively (do an eBay auction or create a blog to find sponsors)
✔ Get everything in writing

✔ Don't give up too soon. Sometimes you may have to kiss a lot of frogs to get a sponsored wedding

Craigslist, Freecycle, eBay, Goodwill and the Salvation Army

If you really want to save some serious cash…check out these resources for great bargains.

The key to finding wedding deals with these methods is to start early and check daily. You may find items from a wedding that never happened. You may also find some items for FREE!

If not for free, you may find some incredible items at a very low price… everything from wedding gowns to ring bearer pillows.

If you do find a dress for example, you will want to factor in the cost of alterations and dry cleaning. Hey, you may get lucky and find your dream dress in your size.

You may have a certain vision for your wedding…but by keeping your mind and your eyes open to other possibilities you can come away with a beautiful wedding without starting off your marriage broke.

Eloping

From the dictionary:

Elope: verb (used without object), e·loped, e·lop·ing.

1. to run off secretly to be married, usually without the consent or knowledge of one's parents.

Today "elope" has a much broader meaning. Many times it means a couple wishes to be married without all of the fanfare or expense of a traditional wedding.

There are many reasons to elope:

- ❀ Wedding Expense - It is easy to spend twenty grand on a wedding. You and your fiancé may want to spend your money more sensibly or you may just not want to start your life together in debt.

- ❀ Dislike attention - Some couples just don't want all the hoopla and ceremony.

- ❀ Want a small wedding - An intimate ceremony declaring your love to each is very appealing to some. Plus you can still have the party afterward.

- ❀ Marrying Once More - You've been there done that and don't feel that all of the "dream wedding" stuff is necessary.

- ❀ Want to marry immediately - Or at least soon. Maybe due to military obligations, job relocation or you're having a baby.

- ❀ Family - Maybe your family is not supporting you. You may have a huge family making a traditional wedding just too much to handle. Maybe you or your family lives overseas.

- ❀ Religion / Culture - There may be some conflict regarding your religious views or cultural or ethnic differences.

- ❀ Peace of Mind - Planning a wedding is stressful, time consuming and expensive. Some people just don't want to go through all of that.

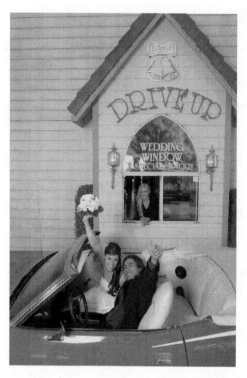

These are all good reasons to elope but on the other hand, if you have always dreamed of your big day...don't give that up. Whatever suits you and you fiancée is the right thing to do.

Index